D0207933

The Ideology of Images
in Educational Media

Hidden Curriculums in the Classroom

The Ideology of Images
in Educational Media

Hidden Curriculums in the Classroom

edited by
Elizabeth Ellsworth
and
Mariamne H. Whatley

Teachers College, Columbia University
New York and London

Randall Library UNC-W

Published by Teachers College Press, 1234 Amsterdam Avenue New York, NY 10027

Copyright © 1990 by Teachers College, Columbia University

All rights reserved. No part of this publication may be reproduced or transmitted in any form or by any means, electronic or mechanical, including photocopy, or any information storage and retrieval system, without permission from the publisher.

Library of Congress Cataloging-in-Publication Data
The Ideology of images in educational media : hidden curriculums in the classroom / edited by Elizabeth Ellsworth and Mariamne H. Whatley.
    p.   cm.
  Includes bibliographical references and index.
  ISBN 0-8077-3044-0 (alk. paper). —ISBN 0-8077-3043-2 (pbk.: alk. paper)
  1. Audio-visual education—United States—Evaluation.
2. Education—United States—Curricula. 3. Teaching—Aids and devices. I. Ellsworth, Elizabeth Ann. II. Whatley, Mariamne H.
LB1043.I34   1990
371.3'35—dc20   90-42057

ISBN 0-8077-3044-0
ISBN 0-8077-3043-2 (pbk.)

Printed on acid-free paper
Manufactured in the United States of America
97 96 95 94 93 92 91 90   8 7 6 5 4 3 2 1

LB
1043
.I 34
1990

Contents

The Ideology of Images
in Educational Media

Hidden Curriculums in the Classroom

Introduction

ELIZABETH ELLSWORTH and MARIAMNE H. WHATLEY

At the 1988 American Educational Research Association (AERA) Annual Meeting in New Orleans, the contributors to this book presented a symposium entitled "Ideology of Images in the Classroom: Educational Film, Television, and Textbook Photographs." At what is considered to be the most important meeting for educational researchers, ours was the only session that sought to question the uses and ideological work of representation in the classroom. At the encouragement of members of the audience, we decided that a collection of these papers would fill an obvious gap in educational literature. In addition, the enthusiasm and support of the audience led to the formation of a new AERA Special Interest Group entitled "Media, Culture, and Curriculum."

Uses of films, television, and photographs in classrooms have a long history and enjoy wide acceptance as welcome and legitimate teaching strategies. Educational media play significant and sometimes primary roles in virtually all curriculums. Yet curriculum theorists and sociologists of education have largely excluded questions of representation from ideological analyses of curriculum materials and classroom practice. Sociologists of education have produced sophisticated and persuasive analyses of how and why textbooks, prepackaged curriculums, and the structure of everyday life in classrooms select some ways of making sense of the world out of the many available, and present them as objective, factual school knowledge. They have argued convincingly that educational theory is not merely the application of objective scientific principles to the concrete study of learning. Rather, it is a political discourse that emerges from specific historical contexts. However, as a field of research, the sociology of education has paid little attention to intersections between media and the curriculum. Research into the ideological work of educational media has been virtually nonexistent. Recently, however, some researchers in education and media studies have begun to raise this issue (Ellsworth, 1987, 1988; Mattleart, 1985; Prendergast & Prout, 1985; Whatley, 1988). Still, the ideological work of images in the classroom remains one of the most hidden of the hidden curriculums. By "hidden curriculum," we are referring to the "tacit teaching to students of norms, values, and dispositions that goes on simply by their living in and coping with the institutional expectations and routines of schools day in and day out for a number of years" (Apple, 1979, p. 14).

One might expect that researchers in the fields of educational communications technology or contemporary media studies would already have taken up such work. Yet, research in educational technology remains preoccupied with questions of how viewers "learn" through media and what isolated "effects" specific media techniques have on the learning process (use of color vs. black and white images, use of moving vs. still images) and has increasingly shifted the focus of the field toward applications in business, industry, and higher education. Some have argued that these preoccupations and this focus are "inappropriate" in light of current crises in public education (Kerr, 1989). The goal of such research is to increase efficiency in meeting educational objectives by increasing predictability and control of the effects of media viewing on the learner. Such research privileges questions of how individuals "process information" from educational media over and above questions about the ideological work of constructing meaning, selecting content, setting objectives, and creating contexts for media use. The concept of information processing as developed within cognitive psychology and applied in educational technology research cannot explain meaning, intent, and significance.

While questions of meaning, intent, and significance are central to contemporary media studies, theorists and critics in television and film studies have largely shunned educational media texts as inadequate or insignificant objects of analysis. As long as debates about auteurs, aesthetics, popularity, and filmic enunciation dominated media studies, the highly formulaic, seemingly banal styles and structures of educational media, and the institutional nature of their use and exhibition, ensured their marginalization. In the last few years, a handful of researchers in media studies have finally begun to extend their analysis to the relation between media and education (Buckingham, 1984; Kuhn, 1985; Lusted & Drummond, 1985; Masterman, 1980, 1985; Richards, 1986). While this new work promises to raise issues crucial to understanding representation in classrooms, it remains grounded in concerns and methodologies most appropriate for discussing the impact of popular culture in the classroom. Questions of the ideological work of mainstream educational media remain unanswered.

This book addresses this significant gap in the otherwise growing literature on hidden curriculums. It does this by posing questions, from a variety of starting points, about the relation between visual representation and the construction of knowledge in educational media. The common problem underlying each chapter is twofold:

- How does the use of visual representation in curriculum materials privilege some ways of knowing over others?
- How do the terms and interests of such privileging relate to the school's role in society?

The authors have approached these questions through current methodologies of ideological analysis developed within media studies.

For the past 20 years, researchers in the field of media studies have used methods of ideological analysis to argue compellingly that conventions of film, video, and photographic representation are not neutral carriers of content. Rather, they are ideological forms that inflect content with particular meanings. Likewise, educational media are not neutral carriers of educational content, and they too are knowledge forms that inflect curricular content with particular meanings and interests. Work within the sociology of education starts from the premise that knowledge is socially constructed and the methods and forms of conveying knowledge shape knowledge itself.

We want to locate within our textual analyses the ways in which the very forms of educational film, video, and photographs operate, intentionally or unintentionally, to privilege some ways of knowing over others. Apple (1982) argues that the key to uncovering the role of ideology in education "is to see its work at the level of form" (p. 139). He demonstrates that, as an analytical category, knowledge form allows the researcher to identify ways in which the level of organization of material functions ideologically as knowledge control. His argument suggests that particular ideological agendas may enter most effectively into schools not at the level of content of educational media, but at the level of the "encoding of technical control into the very basis of the curricular form itself" (p. 149). For example, according to Apple, school curriculums organize our experiences "in ways similar to the passive individual consumption of prespecified goods and services that have been subject to the logic of commodification so necessary for continued capital accumulation in our society" (p. 32).

We extend that argument, and challenge educators to respond to evidence that the ideological effectiveness of official school curriculums is linked to both the logical organization *and* the aesthetic experience of those curriculums—an experience that often includes appeals to aesthetic sensibilities and activates socially constructed expectations of film, television, and photographic viewing. Our efforts to link ideological analysis of representation to a critique of the hidden curriculums of educational media arise from a specific political perspective. We are committed to constructing classroom practices that struggle against the ways that sexism, elitism, racism, and other oppressive formations structure classroom interactions. As a method of interpretation, ideological analysis can identify aspects of educational media production and use that must be changed if this goal is to be met.

Annette Kuhn (1982) offers a definition of ideological analysis that describes the assumptions and processes underlying the analyses in this book, and indicates how such a methodology yields understandings that contribute to the goals stated above. In ideological analysis the objective is to expose the underlying operations of a text by means of a symptomatic reading, that is, attention to a text's silences, gaps, and absences. Ideologies are understood as partial accounts of the world constructed from within particular perspectives, historical contexts, and economic, political, and social interests. They "work" to serve the interests for and from which they have been constructed by offering individuals a perspective on the world, a position from which to make sense of the world and act in it in ways that serve the interests of a particular social position. The perspectives and interests embedded within a particular ideology are presented in texts as if they were natural, given, and those of the individuals being addressed. Because ideologies are partial, they are never seamless, complete, or coherent. Rather, they are characterized by disjunctures, contradictions, "cracks" in their smooth operation. Because openly admitting these interests and contradictions would preclude their being made to appear "natural," ideological operations necessarily remain unconscious, or repressed, elements within texts. For example, class divisions within the United States may be an important "structuring absence" in photographs depicting healthy exercise in health education textbooks, when they assume as given and natural an income capable of supporting the hobby of hang gliding to relieve stress, and address the reader as if she or he were "naturally" middle or upper middle class.

Ideological analysis is therefore more interested in locating and accounting for what is not in a text than what actually is in it. It regards "silences and absences as crucial in structuring the ideological operation of texts" (Kuhn, 1982, p. 85) and generates readings of films that "make them say what they have to say within what they leave unsaid" (Cahiers du Cinema, 1972, p. 9). While every text is part of an ideological system, ideology does not necessarily operate similarly in all texts. Different texts require different methodologies for locating their structuring absences and situating them historically. In general, as Kuhn (1982) describes it, an ideological analysis is a kind of slowing-down of the reading of a text, "a commentary on each segment in turn, an analysis of its underlying operations and a signalling of the processes at work in individual segments and across the text as a whole" (p. 87). However, some analyses may "concentrate on specific moments of the film which are seen as in some sense condensing its ideological processes" (p. 87) and then subject these sequences to in-depth analysis.

This type of analysis serves the political position outlined above when its central concern is how the ideological operations of the educational media in question serve the specific interests of gender, race, class, and so forth. What is made clear are the ways in which histories of marginalized groups within particular historical contexts are systematically absent, repressed, and/or given meanings that undercut those groups, and how the controlling discourses in the texts serve the interests of particular social groups within particular historical contexts.

The first five chapters focus on one medium—educational film. The last two chapters move on to consider two other media, instructional television and textbook photographs. In Chapter 1, "Educational Films Against Critical Pedagogy," Ellsworth introduces a critical framework for analyzing educational films and then applies it to several examples. She argues that teachers committed to constructing classroom practices against racism, sexism, classism, and other oppressive formations must often do so in spite of the curriculum materials, including educational films, available to them. Analyzing the conventions of form and style that typify traditional educational films, she shows that while teachers and students are active producers and negotiators of meaning, the aesthetic conventions of most educational films negate this classroom reality. Ellsworth studies a sample of films produced between 1940 and 1960 to determine the norms that were set in place during the time when the dominant style of educational films became fully established. She then compares these norms with the forms and styles of two contemporary educational films that deal with social issues. This comparison suggests that while some conventions have changed across time, they continue to be employed in ways that actively work against classroom practices intended to engage with the multiple and contradictory social identities present and competing for legitimacy in schools.

In Chapter 2, Barbara Erdman analyzes the form and style of 50 educational films produced between 1930 and 1960 for use in elementary and secondary classrooms. She focuses on the structure of the lesson in teaching films and the interrelationship between instructional intent and educational film form and style. She challenges the commonsense notions that these films simply translate into visual form the pedagogical principles reflected in lesson design. Rather, because these films incorporate formal and stylistic elements from Hollywood feature films and other popular film forms, the viewing experiences they offer often contradict the objectives of the lesson. She argues that it is important for educators to recognize that educational films constitute curricular forms in and of themselves, and that their aesthetic appeals to viewers may either exist harmoniously or conflict with other curricular forms.

In Chapter 3, Mimi Orner focuses on a particular type of educational film known as the "trigger" film. She analyzes the ideological work going on in and through these films in terms of their forms, styles, and uses in classrooms. She examines how the concerns and assumptions embedded within the field of educational psychology and instructional media design relate to the history of trigger films as practices and products. She shows the terms in which trigger films try to provoke discussion among students in classrooms, and why this is significant. She argues that the project of these films is to "trigger" students into a kind of classroom discussion predicated on dominant notions of what constitutes proper behavior and attitudes. The form and style of trigger films construct particular points of view that validate some ways of thinking about provocative topics while ignoring others. Students are invited to take up the positions offered by the film through textual operations that present these positions as if they were the students' own. She questions whether viewers of these films ever actually accept the invitations offered by the text, and challenges the assumption that students are passive consumers of media and are thus "trigger-able."

In Chapter 4, Margot Kennard examines the production of commercially sponsored films for menstruation education. She demonstrates how sponsored educational films can be understood as sites where various and competing ideologies about menstruation are produced, reproduced, and struggled over. Kennard explores two "sites" where knowledge about menstruation is produced, represented, and struggled over: the production of Personal Products' *Growing Up on Broadway*, and of Kimberly-Clark's *Julie's Story*. She challenges commonsense notions about the power of the film's commercial sponsor to determine how menstruation will be represented in the film. The production of *Growing Up on Broadway*, for example, involved a number of different groups representing a variety of backgrounds and interests, including the corporate sponsor, the filmmakers, and the young women portrayed in the film. Kennard demonstrates that the struggle among these groups to inflect the film with meanings that serve their particular interests resulted in a film text that is contradictory and at times threatens the sponsor's commercial project.

In Chapter 5, Bonnie Trudell connects representation in educational films directly to classroom practice. Using ethnographic data, she documents the process by which a film on teenage pregnancy was initially presented to health teachers at a district inservice, and their decision to use it in their classrooms. Her study continues to describe the actual use of that film in one high school health education classroom. She examines the "norms" of sexuality and gender relations with which students are invited to identify, and contrasts them with the actual student response. Her interviews with students allow the further exploration of students' constructions of the film's meanings.

Ann De Vaney analyzes the development of instructional television (ITV) in Chapter 6, and traces the codes inherent in that medium's ubiquitous "talking heads" to their domains of origin. She relates these codes to curriculum development in the 1950s, and argues that they continue to influence the practice of instructional television today. Decisions about ITV form and content excluded input from professional educators and were based on the interests of the administrators of the major sources of funding. As a result, ITV did not address the realities of classroom contexts and has been regarded as a failure. Her analysis of the struggles over defining the conventions of this new educational medium contradicts the popular assumption that it was constrictions of time, budget, and personnel that forced producers to select the "talking head" as the dominant convention for structuring knowledge in ITV.

In Chapter 7, Mariamne Whatley directs an ideological analysis at photographs used in health education textbooks. Her work reveals that, just as educational films draw on Hollywood conventions, these text photographs are similar in image and function to contemporary advertisements, selling "health" by creating readers' dissatisfaction with their own bodies and lifestyles, while creating the desire for those represented in the photographs. The "healthy image" she identifies is very limited, representing a mythical norm (who may, in fact, not be very healthy): white, young, middle class, thin, physically active, and physically abled. Her chapter continues to explore how those people—people of color, and old, poor, fat, and disabled people—left out of the textbooks' "pictures of health" are represented in photographs elsewhere in the texts. Throughout her chapter she develops examples of alternative photographic constructions of "health" that would be more inclusive and in direct opposition to the racist and elitist ideologies underlying current images.

What sets this book apart from approaches in sociology of education is its attention to representation in educational media—a concern that is absent in that field's focus on the social construction of knowledge. Further, it departs radically from the way that researchers in educational technology have viewed educational media as simple and neutral transmitters of reality. By taking seriously the ideological work of films, video, and photographs intended for classroom use, we offer a challenge to both teacher educators and teachers in the schools to respond to these analyses by reconceptualizing classroom practices using mainstream educational media. This might involve multiplying the perspectives from which educational media are interpreted and used in classrooms, and interrupting and disrupting the ideological work of individual media texts.

We have deliberately refused to offer prescriptions for how to change classroom practices using mainstream educational media. There is no one "correct" ideological analysis of any given educational film, video, or photograph, leading to one "correct" use of the text in classrooms. Rather, ideological analysis "may be regarded as a strategic practice" (Kuhn, 1985, p. 8). That is, analyses are judged not for their truth but for their ability to increase our understanding of how educational media, when they are used "uncritically in highly circumscribed ways" (p. 8), delimit what meanings and perspectives can legitimately be taken up in a classroom. For educators committed to including as legitimate within official school knowledge the meanings and perspectives of groups that have been excluded (women and men of color, white women, people with disabilities, lesbians and gay men, Jews, impoverished people, to cite some examples), an understanding of the terms and mechanisms by which educational media exclude these perspectives is necessary for action. The precise actions and the kinds of understandings necessary, however, are profoundly determined by the specific historical, social, institutional, and economic context in which an educator is trying to make a difference. Classroom practices using media to disrupt exclusionary structures of power for the purpose of multiplying "legitimate" perspectives must be constructed in ways appropriate for specific contexts. The question of which silences, absences, and invisibilities in any given text should be "restored" through ideological analysis can be answered only in reference to a particular context of struggle. In fact, ideological analysis itself demands a context of struggle, because without anti-sexist, anti-racist, anti-elitist movements in education, our desire "to question representation in this way could not be articulated, nor would the public or even the private space to do so exist" (Kuhn, 1985, p. 3). Just as ideological analysis is grounded in specific contexts of struggle, decisions about how to use new understandings of educational media generated by ideological analysis must also be made in reference to a particular classroom and its particular participants.

This book, then, offers explorations of the kind of strategic understandings that ideological analyses of educational media make possible. It is intended to contribute to the strategies for interpretation available to educators as they define for themselves what is important to understand about mainstream educational media and what they must do with them in their particular contexts of struggle.

REFERENCES

Apple, M. W. (1979). *Ideology and curriculum.* London: Routledge & Kegan Paul.

Apple, M. W. (1982). *Education and power.* London: Routledge & Kegan Paul.

Buckingham, D. (1984). The whites of their eyes: A case study in response to educational TV. In M. Straker-Welds (Ed.), *Education for a multicultural society* (pp. 137–143). London: Bell & Hyman.

Cahiers du Cinema. (1972). John Ford's *Young Mr. Lincoln. Screen, 13* (3), 5–44.

Ellsworth, E. (1987). Educational films against critical pedagogy. *Journal of Education, 169* (3), 32–47.

Ellsworth, E. (1988). Educational media, ideology, and the presentation of knowledge through popular cultural forms. *Curriculum and Teaching, 3* (1&2), 19–31.

Kerr, S. T. (1989, February). Teachers and technology: An appropriate model to link research with practice. Paper presented at the Annual Conference of the Association for Educational Communications Technology, Dallas, Texas.

Kuhn, A. (1982). *Women's pictures: Feminism and cinema.* London: Routledge & Kegan Paul.

Kuhn, A. (1985). *The power of the image: Essays on representation and sexuality.* London: Routledge & Kegan Paul.

Lusted, D., & Drummond, P. (Eds). (1985). *TV and schooling.* London: British Film Institute.

Masterman, L. (1980). *Teaching about television.* London: Macmillan.

Masterman, L. (1985). *Teaching the media.* London: Comedia.

Mattleart, M. (1985). Education, television, and mass culture: Reflections on research and innovation. In P. Drummond and R. Paterson (Eds.), *Television in transition* (pp. 164–184). London: British Film Institute.

Prendergast, S., & Prout, A. (1985). The natural and the personal: Reflections on birth films in schools. *British Journal of Sociology of Education, 6* (2), 173–182.

Richards, C. (1986). Anti-racist initiatives. *Screen, 27* (5), 74–79.

Whatley, M. H. (1988). Photographic images of blacks in sexuality texts. *Curriculum Inquiry, 18* (2), 137–155.

1
Educational Films Against Critical Pedagogy

ELIZABETH ELLSWORTH

Educational films and television play significant and sometimes primary roles in many curriculums. Yet surprisingly and disturbingly, until very recently educators have excluded them from ideological analyses of curriculum materials and classroom practice.

Within the sociology of education tradition, educational researchers interested in uncovering how official school knowledge is constructed and legitimated have analyzed textbooks, curriculums, classroom practices, and institutional structures. They have demonstrated persuasively that teachers committed to constructing critical pedagogies often must do so in spite of the curriculum materials available to them. Using methods of ideological analysis adapted from literary criticism and critical cultural studies, they have demonstrated, for example, that the content of official school textbooks includes the knowledges of dominant social groups and excludes and delegitimizes the knowledges of subordinate groups (Apple, 1982, 1987). At the level of form, they have shown that the logic of the organization of textbooks and classroom practices encodes technical control, authority, legitimacy, and the "naturalness" of official knowledge into the structures of everyday life in schools (Apple, 1982).

This work gives us a helpful foundation for asking how the forms and content of educational media privilege some ways of knowing over others, and how the terms and interests of such privileging relate to the school's role in society. Researchers interested in the ideology of educational communications technology are, at last, beginning to address these questions (DeVaney Becker, 1989; Ellsworth, 1987, 1988; Kennard, 1987; Orner, 1987).

This chapter reports on research that contributes to that effort. Specifically, I want to focus on how the conventions of visual representation and narrative form found in most educational films contradict the goals of

Reprinted by permission from *Journal of Education*, Volume 169, Number 3, 1987. © Trustees of Boston University liberatory education. I will argue that while teachers and students are active producers and negotiators of meaning, educational films use aesthetic conventions and offer viewing experiences in ways that work against critical pedagogy.

DEFINING CRITICAL PEDAGOGY

My analysis of educational films is located within a view of critical pedagogy that sees a special potential role for media in facilitating liberatory education. In an article entitled "Empowerment as a Pedagogy of Possibility," Roger Simon (1987) offers a useful starting point. Simon argues that all education presupposes and offers a vision of the future and produces "images of that which is not yet" (p. 371). As a social institution, education is implicated in attempts to organize futures according to the dreams of those who have the power to define them. Educators construct for students representations of the world in language and image. "Every time we organize narratives in our classrooms we are implicated in the organization of a particular way of understanding the world and the concomitant vision of one's place in that world and in the future" (p. 377).

"That which is not yet" cannot be observed, accurately predicted, or controlled. Products of the "social imagination" underlying education can only be *represented* in language, images, and narratives. This points to the necessity for educators to understand how representations of the future figure consciously and unconsciously in the language, images, and narratives of curriculums and everyday life in schools. Through representation and narrative, educational media play a central role in education's project of imaging the future and offering students a place to stand in it.

However, as Simon points out, not all visions of the future are benign. In order to evaluate the relationship between traditional conventions of educational film form, style, and narrative and liberatory futures, it is important to make explicit something that is often left unstated in definitions of "progressive education," namely, a guiding cultural politics that specifies what counts as liberating (Kliebard, 1986; Simon, 1987).

Implicit philosophies of progressive education are often grounded in the utopian assumption that we can define universal standards according to which a single perfect future alternative can be designed. The cultural politics guiding my assessment of educational films is one that rejects notions of universal standards and perfection as inherently oppressive. Desirable universal standards and a perfect future are always envisioned from some particular point of view. As a result, they will always be conditioned by the interests and understandings associated with the privileges and limitations experienced in the life-histories of the persons envisioning them. While life-histories are to some extent individual, they are fundamentally determined by social positioning—a person's often contradictory and constantly changing place in the systems of social, economic, political, and ideological differences (Henriques, Hollway, Urwin, Venn, & Walkerdine, 1984).

Social differences that result from the process of social positioning are not themselves inherently or inevitably oppressive. The drawing of boundaries is necessary to make sense of the world and our places in it. But the construction of meaning and social positions is always performed in the interest of perpetuating some sets of relations over others. This "interest" necessarily establishes unequal or contradictory relationships between the social spaces defined by boundaries of difference (Ellsworth & Selvin, 1986; Martin & Mohanty, 1986). We cannot eliminate differences or boundaries, but liberatory education can help us create a *dialogue across differences*, as opposed to the imposition of one group's notion of perfection or universal standards. Gramsci's position on radical art practice is relevant here. Like education, radical art practice offers visions of the future. He argues: "It is not important to decide the form that a radical art practice should take, but very important to specify and work towards the conditions of production that will bring it into being" (Kaplan, 1986, p. 12).

This definition of liberatory education suggests criteria for evaluating whether the kind of viewing experiences offered by conventional educational films facilitate or hinder critical pedagogy. We can ask: What kinds of possible futures and places within them do conventions of educational film image and narrative offer to students? What kinds of relationships do these conventions set up between viewer as "self" and the film's represented "others"? What kinds of relationships do these conventions project between the viewers, knowledge, and action?

UNDERSTANDING THE VIEWING EXPERIENCE

Before analyzing specific films in light of these questions, it is important to explain more fully how conventions of film image and structure offer particular types of viewing experiences. This is central to my argument that the specificity of the ideological effectiveness of educational films lies in the total experience of viewing that film, not simply in the transmission or structuring of this or that subject or content.

By "viewing experience," I am not referring to personally emotional, voluntary, or idiosyncratic responses to the film as stimulus or message.

Rather, I am referring to the viewer's experience of being addressed by the film in ways that invite her or him to take up particular kinds of *physical*, *social*, and *ideological* involvements in the unfolding of the film's story or discourse.

It is worth quoting Len Masterman (1985) at length for a description of this process, which has been called "audience positioning" in cinema studies:

> Texts *attempt to make sense of us*, by offering us positions from which we are invited to see experience in particular ways. The question, "how are we, as audiences, positioned in and by this text?" may be asked of any television program, film, or newspaper and magazine article. What does this question mean? First of all, within the visual media we, as audience members, are compelled to occupy a particular *physical* position by virtue of the positioning of the camera. Identifying and being conscious of this physical position should quickly reveal that we are also being invited to occupy a *social* space. A *social* space is also opened up for us by the text's mode of address, its setting, and its format. Finally the physical and social spaces which we are invited to occupy are linked to *ideological* positions—"natural" ways of looking at and making sense of experience. (p. 229)

Masterman then gives an example of audience positioning in television news:

> As the news opens, we are addressed by a news reader who looks directly at the camera and delivers "the facts." Each viewer is given the role of direct addressee. We cut to a filmed interview. Our position changes. We are no longer directly addressed, but eavesdrop, watch and judge. The different positions assure us that some aspects of experience must be accepted (facts), whilst others (opinions) require our judgment. The highly questionable distinction within journalism between fact and opinion is sewn into the ways in which we are positioned in relation to different aspects of experience. (pp. 229–230)

Thus, as Masterman suggests, to make sense of an educational film on its own terms, the viewer must be able to adopt—if only imaginatively and temporarily—the social, political, and ideological interests that are the conditions for the knowledge it constructs. In this way, the film's discourse seeks to engage the viewer not only in the activity of knowledge construction, but in the construction of knowledge from a particular social, political, and ideological point of view. Thus, "viewing experience" must be seen not as voluntary and idiosyncratic, but as fundamentally relational—a projection of particular kinds of relations between self, others, knowledge, and power.

This is not to suggest that the internal structures and rules of educational film norms *cause* students to have the viewing experiences intended by the filmmakers. Recent audience studies have provided ample evidence that "audiences work upon texts in complex and different ways, just as much as texts work upon audiences. Neither audiences nor texts pre-exist . . . their interactions with one another" (Masterman, 1985, p. 227). Yet for educators interested in linking their students' interpretation of films to the analysis of how social difference becomes defined and used, it remains important to understand how media texts structure and mobilize signs and meanings circulating within the culture in a way that offers viewers a social place to stand within that structure.

In the analysis that follows, I will look specifically at what kind of vision of the future is offered by the educational films I studied. But more important, I will show that the audience positions constructed by dominant conventions of educational film image and narrative invite a type of social involvement in the unfolding of that future that works against liberatory education.

STUDYING EDUCATIONAL FILMS

As part of a larger, two-year research project on the forms, styles, and ideologies of educational film, I analyzed 100 films produced for classroom use between 1930 and 1965. The collection, housed at the American Archives of the Factual Film at Iowa State University in Ames, represents the efforts of major educational film producers during the time when the dominant style of educational films became fully established, and before significant changes in curriculum practices and educational film norms began to take place. For the purpose of this chapter, I selected six study films representative of the range of forms, styles, and topics apparent in the larger sample, and I performed a close shot-by-shot analysis of each. *Social Sex Attitudes in Adolescence* (McGraw-Hill, 1953) and *Car Theft* (Bray-Mar Productions, 1956) are dramatizations with off-screen narrators telling and interpreting the story. *Do I Want To Be a Secretary?* (Coronet Films, 1954) is a dramatization narrated by a character within the story. *School Bus Patrol* (Calvin Productions, 1963) combines dramatization with documentary, with a character/narrator constructing an argument and offering the dramatization as evidence in its support. *We Get Food from Plants and Animals* (McGraw-Hill, 1960) and *Reading Maps* (Encyclopaedia Britannica Films, 1955) frame illustrated classroom-type lectures within minimal dramatizations that insert the information into contexts of human action.

Following Masterman's description of audience positioning, I looked for the ways in which the visual style of each film offers viewers a particular physical position, as indicated by camera placement and movement, in relation to other people and objects in the film. Supplementing Masterman's methodology, I looked additionally for the ways in which the narrative structures of the films solicit from the viewer particular kinds of involvement in the unfolding of the films' stories or discourses. That is, how does the telling of the story encourage us to identify with some of the characters and their points of view, desires, experiences, relations with other characters, and objects of scrutiny—but not with others? I then asked how the physical and narrative positions offered us as viewers open up and invite us to occupy particular *social* positions within race, gender, and class dynamics. Finally, the physical, narrative, and social positions were analyzed in terms of how they are linked to specific *ideological positions*—from which some knowledges are seen as valid and others as invalid.

Positioning the Viewer Physically

Camera placement compels the viewer to occupy a particular *physical* position in relation to characters, objects, and spaces in the film. In classical Hollywood films, this physical position is often associated with that of the film's characters, "anchoring the image in the vision and perspective of one or another character" (Flitterman-Lewis, 1987, p. 194) and positioning the viewer *within* the fictional world. We are moved into and through the space of that world at the sides of its characters. Such physical positioning draws us into the film's fictional world by inviting us to identify with characters' optical points of view, and the fears, desires, and expectations associated with them.

The physical positioning offered to viewers in the educational films studied is quite different. Rather than moving us, at the sides of characters, into and through the space of an autonomous, coherent fictional world, the camera in the study films places the viewer *outside* the worlds represented in the films, from where we are invited to look in. In place of the look from within, we are offered a look from without. Annette Kuhn (1985) has described the kind of camera placement in educational feature films from the early 1900s as "frontal 'tableau' shots" that left narrative space undissected. The camera tended to keep a distance from the action, "sustaining a single angle and point of view even when a close-up or cut-in signals significant detail or emotion" (p. 108). For the most part, this description holds for educational films produced from 1940 to 1960, giving them an old-fashioned, "staged" look when compared with feature films.

The single angle and optical point of view offered to viewers by the types of camera placement Kuhn describes is not free-floating or arbitrary. Rather, it is anchored to the physical position of the narrator. The unseen narrator who appears as a voice-over, ordering and explaining a film's story, stands outside the story, looking in. His[1] direct address to us—on the order of "as you can see . . ."—is like an aside to someone who is positioned next to him on a plane outside of the fictional world of the film. The opening shots of *Social Sex Attitudes in Adolescence,* for example, are frontal, tableau-like views of Bob and Mary's wedding party emerging from a church and posing for photographers. The voice-over of the unseen narrator does not disrupt Bob and Mary's world. They cannot hear him as he says, "Today is a high point in the romance of Bob and Mary. For them the future looks bright." The fact that we do hear him places us outside that world as well. The fact that we see what the narrator describes places us physically at his side.

Narrators/characters who appear on screen and address us directly often move freely between "our space" outside the story and "their space" within it. In *School Bus Patrol,* for example, a dramatization of unsafe school bus practices is interrupted by the appearance of Miss Kenny, a schoolteacher, who sits behind her desk, looks directly at us, and says: "Those were the conditions that used to exist in our school bus operations. . . ." As she describes what she did to remedy the situation, we see flashbacks of her actions, while her voice-over explains them to us. The storekeeper in *We Get Food from Plants and Animals* never addresses us directly, but he turns into the narrator of an illustrated lecture on the sources of food, addressed to his son and a friend. As he tells Johnny and Allen where bananas come from, the image cuts from the grocery story to documentary-like footage of banana harvesting and packing in South America. Here, the narrator/character becomes the motivator of images, and our physical position is controlled by his references to objects and events. While Johnny and Allen cannot see the banana harvest, and the students cannot see Miss Kenny's flashbacks, we can: We leave the fictional world of the characters and enter the expository world of the narrators, their minds' eyes.

As these narrators direct our looking on from the outside, we are offered the physical positions of "all-perceiving" spectators, able to be anywhere and everywhere at once. The views provided us by camera placement and, through association, by the narrators are calculated to *reveal* the nature of objects and characters by rendering them visible. They do so by offering full, frontal, straight-on views of objects and characters held up for our observation, or series of views that break actions or objects down into the parts that determine their nature. These are, of course, conventional translations of techniques of scientific empiricism into film language.

As Masterman argues, the identification of the physical position offered viewers by the camera leads to the recognition that we are also being invited to occupy a *social* space. As we can see from the above description, the educational films studied do not invite us to occupy the *social* space of the stories' fictional characters or the actual people in documentary footage. The narrator is not of that world or its people—which are marked by ignorance, confusion, apathy, and/or mystery. The narrator/camera positioning lifts us out of that world and into the world of the narrator, where we are invited to share with him a social position of knowledge, mastery, and control over people and objects.

As Bill Nichols (1976–77) argues regarding the ideological significance of the narrator's role in documentary films, a narrator's direct address appeals to reason and thereby presumes a center for its own discourse. That center is "the locus of He-Who-Knows, which reciprocally calls the viewer into being as a comparable center or locus, distinguished [from the narrator] by the lack of knowledge which is promised him" (p. 47). The promise of these educational films, then, is that the viewer can become like the narrator. The narrator opens up a space beside him and invites the viewer into it, to become like him.

Positioning the Viewer Through Narrative Structure

Like camera placement, narrative or expository development offers viewers particular positions within the structure of the viewing experience. Such development does this by soliciting from the viewer particular kinds of emotional and cognitive investments in how the story or discourse unfolds.

Regardless of whether the study films borrow the conventions of dramatization, documentary, or classroom lecture, each film takes on a before/after, problem/solution structure. The "before" state may be one of ignorance, apathy, disorganization, or confusion over conflicting information. The narrator's discourse, or the film's story, makes it clear that this "before" state is one of unhappiness, danger, antisocial behavior, disorientation, ineffectuality. The stories or exposition clearly links this undesirable state of affairs to a lack of information or knowledge, through which the narrator's discourse attempts to invoke and gratify a desire to know (Nichols, 1976–77, p. 47). For example, in *We Get Food from Plants and Animals*, because he is ignorant of the complexity of the food chain,

Johnny mistakenly dismisses the grocer's job as unchallenging and thereby alienates his schoolmate, a grocer's son. In *School Bus Patrol*, community apathy about school bus safety is associated with a near-accident. In *Do I Want To Be a Secretary?*, Betty is unable to make a decision about her future because she has not taken an organized approach to studying vocational opportunities. And in *Social Sex Attitudes in Adolescence*, Bob and Mary are confused about their feelings because their parents are telling them one thing, and their peers another. But the kind of knowledge we are invited to desire is not just any kind of knowledge, it is the knowledge of the expert/narrator. We are invited to desire his knowledge because the "after" sequence, which images a potential or actual future in which the "problems" are solved, proves his knowledge is good for us: It works, it is correct, it is more modern, and/or it is morally superior.

The transition from "before" to "after" takes place through the intervention of the expert, who may be an unseen narrator or a parent, teacher, or scientist in the story. In the study films and the larger sample from which they were drawn, the expert is always white. He effects the transition by giving the characters and/or viewers new information, insight into human nature that was previously obscured, or glimpses of the better future awaiting the knowledgeable. Narrator intervention often corrects characters' mistaken understanding of themselves. Narrators consistently speak in declarative, definitive terms, knowing the characters better than they know themselves, defining the future as well as the present. In *Do I Want To Be a Secretary?*, the male vocational counselor/narrator tells Betty: "Next year you will continue to study secretarial work as a career, and you will learn more about how your own interests and abilities can be strengthened." In *Car Theft*, the unseen narrator says: "Sally doesn't know it yet, but if she gets in that car, she's in for a pretty bum rap."

After interventions like this one, the characters in the dramatizations and/or the viewers in the expository films are repositioned into a state of knowledge, commitment, organization, certainty, effectiveness. None of the 100 films that I studied in the larger sample qualifies its guarantee of success to characters or viewers who follow the instructions given in the film, change their attitudes, or use their new knowledge in the proper way modeled for them by the experts or characters. Thus, each of the study films ends "happily." This happens as characters solve their problems, find happiness, are saved from horrible accidents, commit themselves to socially responsible action, or become better organized and more effective. Miss Kenny concludes her narration as follows:

> We teachers as well as the parents are delighted with the way our bus patrol has worked out. The members of the patrol like their work, the bus riders enjoy their rides, the bus drivers do a better job, and the parents feel a lot safer about their children than ever before. Do you have a good school bus patrol at your school? (Calvin Productions, 1963)

Expository films end happily when the object or process under scrutiny is fully explained and viewers are assured that good things will come from their new understanding. For example, in *Reading Maps*, the narrator concludes: "We can visit any place in the world if we know how to read the sign language of maps."

Positioning the Viewer Socially

This problem/narrator intervention/solution/happy-ending structure invites viewers into a *social* position that could be described as that of a son learning at the knee of his father. We are positioned optically and narratively at the side of the already knowledgeable, white, male, paternal narrator, where we enjoy a privileged view of objects and of others, and the certainty of his prediction and control of the characters' or discourses' transition from "before" to "after." Yet we are not addressed by the narrative structure as if we, too, were *already* knowledgeable. We do not already share the narrator's knowledge, certainty, or ability or right to control events in the film. Only at the end of the film are we assured of our ability to share fully the narrator's position. The viewer's transition in social position is from child to adult—in most cases, from son to man. (While the narrator in *School Bus Patrol* is female, Miss Kenny delivers a paramilitary discourse dependent on masculinist approaches to discipline and social control.) *We Get Food from Plants and Animals* offers a most literal example of this social repositioning. A son's respect for his grocer father is threatened when a friend doubts the importance and difficulty of being a grocer. The father offers a lecture, illustrated by documentary cutaways, about the complexity of the food chain. The film ends "happily" as the son accepts his position beside the father/narrator and declares: "I just realized something, Dad. If I take over the business someday, I've got a lot to learn. I want people to think I'm just as smart as you are."

Here information about the food chain is organized through the logic of patriarchal and capitalistic relations between fathers and sons. The happy vision of the future that results is one in which those relations are perpetuated and celebrated. Obviously, the terms in which the "problem" of the film is posed (in this case, a son's desire to follow in the father's footsteps, threatened by the son's ignorance of the father's intelligence) project the conditions for what will count as an appropriate solution or happy ending. This method of defining the problem circularly so as to point to a single appropriate "solution" is one means by which the solutions (futures) offered by the films are made to seem inevitable. Part of that circularity is a structuring of narrative and exposition to imply that the facts of the problematic situation itself contain the logic of what should be done. For example, given the facts of adolescent development, as told by the narrator in *Social Sex Attitudes in Adolescence*, Bob and Mary's behavior is "obviously" normal, healthy, and to be expected. Therefore, the solution to the problem of how to parent adolescents is to imitate the behavior of Bob and Mary's successful parents. In *Do I Want To Be a Secretary?*, the film title's question is answered in the affirmative when the facts of Betty's aptitude tests turn out to be congruent with the facts of a secretary's job description. In *We Get Food from Plants and Animals*, the facts of the food chain as revealed in the father's lecture are so complex and crucial to human life that it is obvious that father must be intelligent and his job must be challenging, important, and worth carrying on.

Yet the solutions (futures) in the study films are not in fact inevitable. They present images of some types of solutions and happiness, and withhold images of others. In *Social Sex Attitudes in Adolescence*, happiness comes to Bob and Mary when they accept the middle-class Christian values of their parents. It comes to the grocer's son in *We Get Food from Plants and Animals* when he accepts his father's social position as his own and wishes to follow in his father's entrepreneurial footsteps. It comes to innocent victims in *Car Theft* when youths respect private property and accept middle-class values. It comes to Betty in *Do I Want To Be a Secretary?* when she accepts traditional gender roles and seeks to succeed in male-defined terms. It comes to children and parents in *School Bus Patrol* when the patrol vanquishes the danger of living in the modern world through military-like control, precision, and obedience. It comes to travelers in *Reading Maps* when they master and practice conventions of communication originally designed to facilitate commerce and efficiency. In these films, the future is a projection of the currently dominant social formation and its supporting ideologies onto emerging situations. More specifically, youth culture is seen as the emergent source of new and competing meanings, values, and practices (like sexual experimentation, jazz music, nontraditional aspirations, modernity) that must be incorporated back into the dominant adult culture (Williams, 1977). The study films make incorporation seem imperative by characterizing youth culture as dangerous to personal and public safety. Children's uncontrolled play in the school bus distracts the driver in *School Bus Patrol*, for example, while young men's ideas of excitement lead to the death of a girl in *Car Theft*. They also make youth culture appear excessive and extreme: Popular jazz music accompanies drinking and necking in a parked car in *Social Sex Attitudes in Adolescence*, and the young men in *Car Theft* not only steal a car, but drive it wildly and recklessly.

The study films thus offer a viewing experience that I would describe as paternalistic. That is, conventions of representation and narrative structure project physical, social, and ideological positions of protection, control, certainty, and the guarantee of unqualified success in solving the problems and knowing the objects under scrutiny, if only viewers acquire the white male narrator's information and use it properly, according to the behaviors modeled by the film's characters. A paternalistic audience positioning, of course, works against the liberatory education I described above. It offers viewers a place within a single, static, seemingly perfect future—represented by a white male adult—that has resolved any contested voices into a single, objective, and correct one. The conditions of the production of this voice are hidden and are not to be part of the education of viewers.

While the films occasionally admit alternatives to the experts' understanding of a situation through voices of other characters, they are already subordinated to the preferred understanding of the expert. In *Car Theft*, for example, the boys define stealing as "just having fun." Yet long before the car chase with police leads to the death of a small girl, the boys' definition of what is happening in the film is rendered suspect by the use of disturbing camera angles, ominous music, and the narrator's dismissive or corrective tone of voice.

The study films thus attempt to place viewers in specific relationships to knowledge, action, and the film's represented "others." Experience and social reality are rendered univocal, and the nature of this voice can be known with certainty through objective observation. Alternative voices are mistaken, ignorant, or morally deficient. Outcomes of action based on objective observation can be predicted and controlled, and such prediction and control enhance our chances of success, safety, and happiness. What counts as success, safety, and happiness emerges logically from the facts we uncover. Education lifts us out of the worlds of the mistaken, ignorant, or morally deficient (represented as "Others" in educational films) and makes it possible for us to share the social status of white male scientist-narrators.

Thus viewers are not encouraged to understand themselves relationally, but to assume a position at the center—the norm from which all "others" are defined. Nor are they encouraged to communicate across social differences for the purpose of arriving at knowledge as historically "justified belief," through "productive disagreement" within and across communities. Instead, knowledge is defined as certainty arrived at through the search for correspondence between external reality and its representation in language (Beyer, 1986, p. 122).

THE MORE THINGS CHANGE

Since 1960, some conventions of narration in educational films have begun to change. Influences from cinema verite and television documentary styles, along with the cultural upheavals brought on by the civil rights, anti-war, environmental, and feminist movements, have rejected the position of central white male scientist-narrators as privileged sources and enunciators of knowledge. A detailed analysis of how educational films have modified conventions of representation and narration since 1960, in response to challenges to authority and official school knowledge, is beyond the scope of this study. Yet a quick comparison of two contemporary educational films with the study films analyzed above suggests that while some narrative conventions have changed, others remain intact and continue to act as barriers to liberatory education.

As examples, let us look briefly at *Sex, Drugs and AIDS* (1986), produced by O. D. N. Productions for New York Public Schools, where it is currently mandatory viewing for high school seniors, and widely distributed across the United States; and *Why Is It Always Me?* (1983), produced by MTI Teleprograms, Inc.

The classical conventions of the single, central, and authoritative male enunciator of knowledge are absent in both of these films. *Sex, Drugs, and AIDS* is narrated by Rae Dawn Chong, a young Asian and black woman, familiar to young audiences from her appearances in popular films like *Fame*. She sits cross-legged in casual, stylish dress and speaks directly to the audience in a manner that suggests she is like her audience, because she finds these topics almost as difficult to talk about as she supposes her audience would. Her narration is shared by other voices in the film—those of AIDS victims who address us directly; high school students who dramatize a discussion among themselves about sex, drugs, and AIDS in a gymnasium; a brother of a gay AIDS victim, who addresses us directly with the story of his brother's illness; and an MTV-like sequence of images of "safe" casual physical contact.

In *Why Is It Always Me?* a dramatization of two white junior high school boys having a scuffle over a library book is interrupted by an unseen male narrator who addresses one of the boys directly: "Well, Mike, it looks like it happened again, you got into trouble. You just aren't making good decisions. It looks like learning problem-solving steps might help you." As in television commercials, in which a male voice breaks into the fictional world of a housewife and stops her from using the wrong cleanser, Mike stops, looks directly at the camera/narrator/viewer, and talks back to the narrator. Later he himself becomes a narrator of a sequence in which his voice-over explains fantasy scenes that depict what he imagines he needs to solve problems effectively. (This includes luck, physical strength to coerce his adversaries, and "smarts.") Mike even questions the unseen narrator's authority: "Can you guarantee this will work?" and "You're so smart, you've got all the answers, *you* tell me what to do."

At first glance, this sharing of the enunciation of knowledge among several characters in the films, and the control of the films' discourses by an Asian and black woman or white adolescent boy, seem to offer a less hierarchical, not necessarily white, not necessarily adult male social position to the viewers. But even a cursory analysis shows otherwise. In *Sex, Drugs, and AIDS*, Chong's is the controlling discourse that defines the danger to teens and the steps they should take to protect themselves. She offers scientific and medical "facts." The other narrators provide corroboration, evidence, and emotional hooks to win assent to Chong's presentation of the facts.

In addition, teachers concerned with using *Sex, Drugs, and AIDS* to facilitate dialogue among teenagers must ask what kind of social position the film's representation and narrative structure offer teenage blacks. Its narrator is black and Asian, and one of the testimonials is given by a black woman who says she got AIDS from her partner and passed it on to her baby. According to data from the 1987 International Conference on AIDS held in Washington, DC, people contracting AIDS in the United States through heterosexual contact are disproportionately black women whose partners are intravenous drug users. The fact that the film's IV drug users are white, as are the young women discussing birth control and "safe sex," avoids a stereotypical connection of these issues to the black community. However, it also avoids dealing with the realities of AIDS as a health concern for blacks, involving special economic and historical pressures that have led to high numbers of teenage pregnancies, IV drug use, and inadequate access to health and prenatal care in urban black communities. As a result, viewers may be offered the physical position of a black woman looking in on the issues of the films—but it is the social and ideological position of someone outside the teenage, urban, black communities that the film tries to appeal to.

A similar contradiction can be seen in *Why Is It Always Me?* While Mike motivates the images in the fantasy sequence of the film, his version of the right way to solve problems is clearly and immediately subordinated to the white male off-screen voice. The narrator responds to Mike's fantasy with: "Hold on Mike, you're making a big mistake. You don't need to depend on those things to solve your problems." The rest of the film depicts Mike's transitions from his misconceptions to his agreement that the narrator's way is best.

Scientific empiricism and the guarantee of success are solidly in place in these two films. Chong speaks with declarative, definitive assurance that her facts are correct, and that a knowledge of those facts can make teenagers safe. The film concludes with Chong implying that the issues have been covered completely and viewers now have the facts they need to prevent themselves from getting AIDS. While the unseen narrator of *Why Is It Always Me?* concedes that he cannot *guarantee* success with his problem-solving technique, the story shows Mike's unqualified success in applying it. The technique is even labeled "IDEAL" (for the steps: Identify, Describe, Evaluate, and Learn) which, the narrator explains, is an appropriate way to help remember the steps because they are "the ideal way to solve problems—any problems."

TOWARD A LIBERATORY EDUCATION

As Beyer (1986) argues, education has been defined as an instrumental process obsessed with solving specific, immediate, detailed problems. This orientation has more to do with a search for appropriate techniques, a concern with instrumental rationality, than with a commitment to social action requiring ethical know-how. In the study films, a problem solved constitutes the proof of valid knowledge. In the cultural politics I described above, however, the forms of life and alternative narratives that result from the practice of liberatory education constitute the final arbiters of knowledge. While the conventions of educational films invite students to take up social and ideological positions of the white, male, middle-class scientist/problem solver, critical educators can construct other social positions within their classrooms, which are real material sites of social relations. Simon (1987) suggests that this can be done through "storytelling, literature, and nonhierarchical classroom relationships which offer a variety of narratives demonstrating other possibilities for empowerment beyond the control and oppressive manipulation of others" (p. 36).

I have argued that criteria for evaluating forms of life and alternative

narratives produced within liberatory pedagogies cannot be specified outside the contexts of specific classrooms. It is clear, however, that educational media producers must stop creating images and narratives that invite viewers exclusively into physical, social, and ideological positions of
"He (white, patriarch, scientist, expert)-Who-Knows (with certainty, from
the center)." Rather, the framework for a critical pedagogy outlined at the
beginning of this chapter challenges educational media producers to image futures that offer viewers a different position. This position could be
expressed in various ways: "she or he who knows something that is necessary, but never sufficient for defining appropriate social action"; "she or
he whose knowledge is socially constructed, always partial, changing, and
a product of unconscious as well as conscious processes"; or "she or he
whose decisions about social action can be made only as a result of dialogue across differences with other social actors."

NOTE

1. Narrators in the study films and in the larger sample of educational films
are almost always male, even when the subject of the film is traditionally associated with girls or women. For this reason, I will use "he" when referring to
generic narrators.

REFERENCES

Apple, M. (1982). *Education and power.* London: Routledge & Kegan Paul.
Apple, M. (1987). *Teachers and texts: A political economy of class and gender
    relations in education.* London: Routledge & Kegan Paul.
Beyer, L. (1986). The reconstruction and appropriation of Pierre Bourdieu's anal-
    ysis of social and cultural reproduction. *Journal of Education, 168* (2), 113–
    135.
Bray-Mar Productions (Producer). (1956). *Car theft* [Film].
Calvin Productions (Producer). (1963). *School bus patrol* [Film].
Coronet Films (Producer). (1954). *Do I want to be a secretary?* [Film].
De Vaney Becker, A. (1989). ITV and the talking head. *Educational Technology,
    27* (10), 35–40.
Ellsworth, E. (1987). Fiction as proof: Critical analysis of the form, style and
    ideology of educational dramatization in films. In *Proceedings of selected re-
    search paper presentations at the 1987 convention of the Association for
    Educational Communications and Technology Sponsored by the Research
    and Theory Division.* Atlanta.
Ellsworth, E. (1988). Educational media, ideology, and the presentation of

knowledge through popular cultural forms. *Curriculum and Teaching,* 3(1&2), 19–31.

Ellsworth, E., & Selvin, A. (1986). Using transformative media events for social education. *New Education, 8* (2), 70–77.

Encyclopaedia Britannica Films (Producer). (1955). *Reading maps* [Film].

Flitterman-Lewis, S. (1987). Psychoanalysis, film, and television. In R. Allen (Ed.), *Channels of discourse* (pp. 172–211). Chapel Hill: University of North Carolina Press.

Henriques, J., Hollway, W., Urwin, C., Venn, C., & Walkerdine, V. (1984). *Changing the subject: Psychology, social regulation, and subjectivity.* London: Methuen.

Kaplan, C. (1986). *Sea changes: Culture and feminism.* London: Verso.

Kennard, M. (1987, May). *1947—The sanitary products industry enters the classroom: How a commercially sponsored film became official school knowledge.* Paper presented at Society for Cinema Studies Conference, Montreal.

Kliebard, H. (1986). *The struggle for the American curriculum, 1893–1958.* London: Routledge & Kegan Paul.

Kuhn, A. (1985). *The power of the image: Essays on representation and sexuality.* London: Routledge & Kegan Paul.

Martin, B., & Mohanty, C. T. (1986). Feminist politics: What's home got to do with it? In T. de Lauretis (Ed.), *Feminist studies/Critical studies* (pp. 191–212). Bloomington: Indiana University Press.

Masterman, L. (1985). *Teaching the media.* London: Comedia.

McGraw-Hill Book Co. (Producer). (1960). *We get food from plants and animals* [Film].

McGraw-Hill Book Co. (Producer). (1953). *Social sex attitudes in adolescence* [Film].

MTI Teleprograms, Inc. (Producer). (1983). *Why is it always me?* [Film].

Nichols, B. (1976–77). Documentary theory and practice. *Screen, 17* (4), 34–38.

O.D.N. Productions (Producer). (1986). *Sex, drugs, and AIDS* [Film].

Orner, M. (1987, May). *Films to make students talk: Trigger films and the construction of knowledge.* Paper presented at Society for Cinema Studies Conference, Montreal.

Simon, R. (1987). Empowerment as a pedagogy of possibility. *Language Arts, 64* (4), 370–382.

Williams, R. (1977). *Marxism and literature.* Oxford: Oxford University Press.

2
The Closely Guided Viewer: Form, Style, and Teaching in the Educational Film

BARBARA ERDMAN

Innovations in educational technology continue to be embraced with enthusiasm by the education profession in the perhaps mistaken belief that the lessons offered by media are merely a substitution or direct expansion of lessons offered through older methods. An early article by Charles Gramet (1934) describing the production of an educational film reveals this assumption:

> Planning a motion picture lesson is very much like planning any other.
> 1) We first select the topic.
> 2) To get the interest of our . . . pupils, most lessons require motivation. . . .
>   The interest must be in the subject or problem that is being studied.
> 3) The selection of material depends upon the aim of the lesson. . . . Select
>   then, the ideas or concepts that are to be presented in the lesson and plan
>   your film around these. . . .
> 4) The film lesson (as in every other lesson) should conclude with a general-
>   ization, review or application. (p. 5)

If educational media producers are also guided by the same assumption about instruction and media, we would expect that the instructional motive expressed through an educational medium would act as the organizing principle of design so that all educational communications would share a characteristic style of presentation and common organizing principles directly related to prevailing pedagogical techniques. In fact, however, the styles of presentation across educational media forms such as film, television, and computer software vary dramatically and depart significantly from concurrent pedagogical practices, such as prescriptions for how to structure classroom lessons.

Educational researchers have generated little understanding about what has remained constant and what has altered, across time and between technologies, in the design of mediated lessons. Without a body of critical and historical literature to refer to, educators today may assume that the norms for the design of educational media can be traced to widely accepted theories of instructional design that structure mediated lessons to the needs of learners and hierarchically organize the objectives of instruction. But theories of what is now known as the design of instructional media were not available much before 1960, while one of the earliest forms of educational technology, educational films, were produced in great numbers from the early 1920s.

Obviously, other strategies for making formal and stylistic choices must have guided early producers of teaching films. These strategies may have been aesthetic criteria imposed by film directors who learned their craft outside the field of education, or practices carried over from radio and textbooks. They may also have come from the same beliefs about good teaching that guided classroom teachers.

An overwhelming number of studies conducted on educational film have addressed and continue to address concerns of specific presentation techniques—vocabulary, pacing, and so forth—in an attempt to identify how these individual techniques affect learning. More recently, education researchers have come to recognize that media experiences impose structural and processing requirements on learners (Jonassen, 1984), and much recent educational technology research is concerned with cognition in an attempt to understand these requirements. However, to gain insights into the educational media experience it is necessary to understand something about the film medium itself, viewer expectations, and wider relationships of the medium within the culture.

Sless (1981) reminds us that "education is parasitic on the modes of communication available in our culture" (p. 41). Educational media forms are dependent on popular culture forms for aesthetic style and production techniques. Educational films, for example, draw form and style from the dominant modes of film making. Educational dramatizations use traditional Hollywood techniques of narrative development (Ellsworth, 1987). Teaching films, designed as curriculum-specific, self-contained classroom lessons, also use techniques of cinematography and editing that are familiar in popular films. But within each of these educational film genres, the films adapt the stylistic qualities and narrative forms of the dominant modes of film making for their own educational projects, creating in the process educational film forms and styles with their own characteristics.

The kind of learning experiences made possible and impossible when students interact with each educational communication medium depends on the intersection between the technical and stylistic choices inherent within the medium, whatever conventions of style have already been established by use of that medium in schools (as well as by the broader use of that medium within the culture), and the requirements of prevailing pedagogical form and educational content. How the aesthetic formal and stylistic characteristics of film and the norms of its usage interact to determine the form of instruction experienced by students and teachers using that technology has not been defined. Without an understanding of these interactions and constraints, instructional media scholars have no preliminary understanding or model of instructional film in which to ground criticism and guide film production and use.

I will address this historical, theoretical, and critical gap by focusing on the intersection between form, style, and instructional intent. The main thrust of my work is to provide a descriptive model of teaching films produced between 1930 and 1960 by analyzing how instructional intent influences film form and style in a sample of such films. I have confined my analysis to films produced between 1930 and 1960 because this period followed the introduction of the 16mm film and sound technology widely used in the teaching film. It includes the years when demands for educational films were the heaviest, and preceded the influence on many educational film producers of a new media form, broadcast television. This could be called the "classical period" of educational films, during which norms were established and shared across the industry. While it is not within the scope of my study to address issues of cognition and aesthetic perception, I will necessarily suggest at several points how the structure and style of teaching films encourage specific activities on the part of the viewer.

I make several assumptions. The first is that teaching films were created and viewed within a film culture dominated by Hollywood. In order to be intelligible to audiences, teaching films in the United States drew from a range of forms and production styles commonly used in popular cinema. The second assumption is that producers of teaching films were aware of work being done by others in the field, and that a general practice of educational film production existed. The commonalities of form and style identifiable within the classification of the teaching film constitute a norm and apply generally to all teaching films produced during the period of the study.

After viewing 90 films from the study collection in the American Archives of the Factual Film at Iowa State University at Ames, Iowa, I chose 45 films for the preliminary study. From this sample, 15 films, which are the most representative of the range of form and style, were selected for more detailed analysis.

Each of the films was analyzed using the formalist method defined in the work of Bordwell, Staiger, and Thompson (1985) and Bordwell and

Thompson (1986). They offer a model for categories of film analysis based on principles of form and style. The form of a film refers to its overall thematic arrangement and the general system of all relationships among the parts. Film form, in its broadest sense, is the basic structure of the total system that makes up a film. Style in a film refers to the repeated and salient uses of the techniques of the film medium characteristic of that particular film. Cinematic techniques include scenic elements of setting, costume and make-up, lighting, and figure movement; framing elements of camera angle, camera height, and camera movement; and all aspects of editing and sound. The unified, developed, and significant use of particular technical choices creates a system within a film, which is called its style. Norms of film style are established by identifying a pattern of stylistic features that can be regarded as typical for a film genre. The two systems of form and style work together in the film. The narrative or nonnarrative formal system provides a structure that interacts with stylistic techniques to make the total form that the viewer perceives as a film.

Using a shot-by-shot analysis of the visual and audio tracks, I examine the formal and stylistic elements present in each film, identify pedagogical principles within the design and content, and discuss the relation between the formal and stylistic elements and pedagogy. I address this aspect by comparing the films with prescriptions of lesson design from the period of the films' production to determine whether the logic that underlies instructional theory also underlies teaching film form and style. Thus, my study looks at the ways educational film producers utilized production opportunities available through the already established film medium, in conjunction with widely established prescriptions of instructional design, to create the first educational media form designed for broad distribution and independent use.

THE ORGANIZATIONAL STRUCTURE OF THE TEACHING FILM

Film viewers understand that a film is not a random collection of elements. The different parts of a film relate to one another within a dynamic system called form. A viewer's perception of form comes from cues within the film and is based on prior viewing and wider cultural experiences (Bordwell & Thompson, 1986). The major element of the form that the viewer perceives in a film is its organization or structure. For example, the system of organization in a narrative film comes from the film's story. Viewers differentiate among different types of film forms, and each film genre, narrative or nonnarrative, calls upon different viewing conventions and cues different types of expectations in the viewer. Correspondingly, the type of organizational structure chosen by the film maker will relate to his or her purposes and to the choices available in production and cultural contexts. My interest is in establishing to what extent the teaching film is structured by methods of lesson design authorized by literature on educational theory and practice, and to what extent it provides its own type of learning experiences that may at times undercut authorized notions of lesson design and at times support them. To do this I need to clearly define the organizational structure of the teaching film and to look at the pedagogical elements within that structure to see if it, in turn, creates a lesson form that is unique to teaching films. Defining the formal development in the films through the method of film "segmentation" allows me to analyze film structure. Bordwell and Thompson (1986) discuss segmentation as follows:

> A segmentation is simply a written outline of the film that breaks it into its major and minor parts. . . . Segmenting a film enables us not only to notice similarities and differences among parts; a breakdown makes it easier to plot the overall progression of the form. (p. 39)

The structure of the teaching film revealed through segmentation can then be compared with the organization of the traditional lesson.

THE TRADITIONAL LESSON

For the purposes of this study, I identified the form of the traditional lesson from literature on pedagogical theory and practice published between 1898 and 1959. I included literature published prior to the period of the study films because although contemporary textbooks reflect the latest theories of teaching, actual classroom practice changes more slowly. Schools of education rarely adopt new theories of pedagogy on a widespread basis; many schools continue to prepare teachers in traditional methods. Lesson designs described in teaching methods texts prior to the production period of the study films are as likely to be an indication of classroom practice as those published at the time of the films' production. To identify the form of a lesson, I looked for elements that were common and statements that were consistent across descriptions of lesson organization in literature intended for the preparation of teachers.

A comparison of the Herbartian five steps of a lesson, first defined in the late nineteenth century (Dodd, 1898), with lesson plan descriptions in teaching methods texts through 1959 indicates that theories about the proper components and sequencing of instruction changed very little since they were first defined by the Herbartians. The organization of a lesson from later decades correlates closely to the Herbartian steps.

Based on the principles common to descriptions of lesson organization in the literature that I surveyed, the traditional lesson is a progression of interactions between teacher, students, and subject material, designed and directed by the teacher, and occurring within a specified time period, for the purpose of presenting specific new material to students and evaluating their comprehension and application. The steps of the traditional lesson are

1. Presenting lesson objectives to students
2. Assisting students in recall of prior relevant learning
3. Motivating students through introduction of new material
4. Presenting material and guiding learning by association and demonstration
5. Reviewing
6. Directing student participation and application
7. Evaluating student learning and/or performance

THE LESSON IN THE TEACHING FILM

An analysis of the pedagogical organization in the teaching films studied reveals that the lesson is modeled on traditional lesson design, but not without substantial modifications. From my sample, it was possible to characterize the steps of the film-lesson in the following way:

1. Prologue
2. Presentation of lesson materials, including demonstration or application of concepts
3. Summary or conclusion

Prologue

The teaching film as a form alters the traditional lesson in several significant ways. It excludes both the presentation of lesson objectives and recall of prior learning, and begins with step three of the traditional lesson, a general introduction of the film topic. In this process it excludes the preliminary interaction with subject material that is part of preparing students for new learning experiences. The film makes no assumptions about students' prior learning in the subject area and does not acknowledge that motivation for watching the film is based on the viewer's need or desire to add to prior knowledge. Instead, the film attempts to base the motivation for film viewing on the appeal of the material. Each film includes introductory material to identify the topic, attract the attention of the viewer, and verify the significance of the topic in the world at large and in the life of the viewer. In the absence of the usual motivation, the establishment of significance is achieved through stylistic techniques and rhetorical devices.

The audio portion of the introduction most often contains superlative statements such as "glaciers gouge out deep valleys on the flanks of massive mountains" (Encyclopaedia Britannica Films, 1935). In films produced after 1945, stimulating music usually accompanies the title material and often continues throughout an introductory statement such as, "thousands of ships carrying over 45 million tons of cargo pass through this area each year, saving thousands of miles and hundreds of hours on their sea journeys" (Coronet Films, 1958). Dramatic cinematography and fast-paced editing often accompany the introductory narration.

To provide additional motivation for watching, the introductory material often includes one or two brief references to the personal needs or experiences of the viewer. For example, "How much do you know about trains?" (Young America Films, 1944), or "Food makes people well and happy" (General Pictures Productions, 1947), or "Our breakfast toast is made by red-hot wires in the electric toaster" (Encyclopaedia Britannica Films, 1943). These comments function as a method of attracting the viewer's attention, making the viewer personally identify with the content, and increasing his or her interest in watching. The introduction presents motives for learning based on appeal and personal needs. This is in contrast to classroom lessons in which "a lively discussion of the introduction should follow its presentation" (Wells, 1951, p. 136), and students are motivated through the assistance of the teacher to "independent thinking and analysis of the material . . . to find new implications in the subject matter under discussion" (Strayer, Frasier, & Armentrout, 1936, p. 214).

Presentation of the Lesson

After the introduction, the major part of the film presents the lesson material through a lecture/demonstration format. Information is presented in clearly delineated steps, progressing from simple to more complex concepts or processes. In contrast to the traditional lesson, in the film-lesson there is no student participation or application following the presentation of lesson material. Vicarious experiences are offered instead,

through demonstration or often by showing characters in the film applying the principles of the lesson. In later films the film participant is a
school-age child. For example, in *Simple Machines: The Inclined Plane
Family* (Encyclopaedia Britannica Films, 1959b) a boy named Mark, following the directions of the narrator, applies the principles of pyramid
building by stacking bricks and then appears in a lab setting to carry out
demonstrations that illustrate concepts of the inclined plane. The content
of the audio narration increases the vicarious nature of the viewing experience. The narrator addresses the viewer directly, creating the feeling
that the viewer is a participant in the situation that he or she is viewing.
For example, the narrator in *Reading Maps* (Encyclopaedia Britannica
Films, 1955) says, "Now to use this map, we have to read all the signs
shown on it. First, the scale. The scale tells us . . ."; and the narrator in
The Steam Engine (Young America Films, 1944), says "Now if we closed
both the valves and then cooled the container, the steam would condense
back into water. But we would find that. . . ."

Conclusion

Another way that the teaching film alters the traditional lesson is the
exclusion of a review and teacher evaluation at the end. Instead, the film-
lesson ends quite abruptly with a recapitulation of the topic; for example,
"And that's the story of the steam engine" (Young America Films, 1944).
Sometimes it ends with a very brief review such as, "In this film we have
seen how the ear changes vibrations in air molecules into nerve impulses
that we call sounds" (Encyclopaedia Britannica Films, 1949). Any evaluation of learning from the film-lesson takes place outside the film experience.

Like popular or entertainment works in the medium it appropriates,
the teaching film exists as a self-contained system. The requirements of
the film medium for completeness and unity of form conflict with the
traditional lesson form, which requires continuous interactions between
students, teacher, and lesson material, and an evaluation at lesson closure. The lesson in the film is incomplete because of the film's formal
conventions of closure and unity.

STYLE IN THE TEACHING FILM

The organizing structure of the lesson provides one formal system in
the teaching film. Style, the system that organizes film techniques, such
as cinematography, editing, and sound, provides a second. During the

process of making a teaching film, producers must decide which of the available film techniques to use. The techniques they choose provide both the aesthetic experience of the film and shape its lesson structure. These two systems interact to create meaning within the total film.

To analyze film style, one identifies salient or prominent techniques, traces patterns of techniques within the film, and looks for ways in which techniques reinforce patterns of organization and for ways that style may function in its own right. The term *style* may be used to describe the characteristic use of techniques by a single filmmaker or a group of filmmakers (Bordwell & Thompson, 1986). I identified the techniques that were most common to the films studied. I then analyzed how these choices supported the lessons in the films and whether they took on a stylistic function on their own.

Cinematic Techniques

The majority of the visual content in all of the films in the study group is the demonstration of processes, such as electrical energy or erosion, or the illustration of concepts such as the inclined plane. Producers of teaching films were compelled to find camera techniques that would display the lesson content clearly; in the majority of the films, they turned to special techniques such as animation, superimposed images and graphics, and time-lapse and microscopic photography. About 90 percent of the films I looked at contain some special cinematic techniques. Although no film is entirely animated, about a quarter of the films depend very heavily on animation and graphic techniques such as superimposed labels and arrows in a major part of their content. These two techniques can be considered as typical of the teaching film. Animation and other special techniques add substantially to the illustrative capabilities of the films. Concepts such as fertilization and the movement of ions can be illustrated with precision. Use of special cinematographic techniques adds significantly to the visual variety of the films as well. Some of the films employ specific techniques in ingenious combinations, and in some of the films these techniques become a stylistic motif. For example, in *The Steam Engine* (Young America Films, 1944) a moving arrow appears repeatedly throughout the development of the lesson to guide the viewer's attention to the movement of steam, the force of pressure, the direction of pistons, and the turning of wheels. The viewer begins to expect its guiding presence. However, even in films with a substantial number of techniques, the techniques do not draw attention away from the lesson; the variety they offer reinforces, rather than diminishes, attention to the lesson.

At the same time, the shot scale in the film-lesson is dominated by close-ups in which the scale of an object such as a microscope is relatively large or completely fills the screen, and extreme close-ups in which a small part of an object or an entire very small object such as an eardrum fills the screen. While medium shots are also used, it is the close-up that communicates the majority of the lesson material. A major portion of many of the films consists of long series of close-ups and extreme close-ups. Mobile framing in the form of camera movement, such as pans and tracking, is seldom used, even in animated sequences. Instead, a change in framing is usually achieved by cutting to a new camera position. Surprisingly, zooms in or out are rarely used, in spite of the conventional belief in their ability to focus attention. The film producers may have chosen static framing for reasons of technical economy and efficiency. Mobile framing involves time—it takes more time to pan to a new camera position than to cut from one shot to another—and is therefore a less concise method of illustration. Mobile framing also tends to expand information about an object and its surrounding space as new perspectives are revealed. It encourages interpretation on the part of the viewer and, therefore, as a technique offers less control over viewer understanding of visual material. The prevalence of static framing in the teaching film increases the effect of precisely directed visual attention; the viewer's eye has no opportunity to wander into the surrounding environment and away from the intended subject.

The cinematic techniques employed for illustrative and demonstrative purposes in the teaching film support its teaching function by constructing a film style dominated by special effects techniques and an intimate shot scale. As a lesson form the film becomes a concisely controlled display compelling close visual attention. The lesson in the teaching film offers opportunities for observation beyond those available in most classrooms. At the same time, the form of the film presents an experience in which, unlike a classroom lesson, there is no opportunity to slow the information to allow viewers to reflect and assimilate.

Editing

Editing, the coordination of one shot with the next, includes methods of joining shots—cuts, fades, and dissolves—and the aesthetic juxtaposition of shots. The continuity editing system was designed to control the potentially disunifying force of editing. Continuity editing establishes techniques to ensure a sense of flow from shot to shot, both to tell a story coherently and for aesthetic unity. Teaching films adhere to the most basic continuity editing technique—maintaining a consistent camera position in relation to subjects—but their adherence to other techniques of continuity editing is tenuous. Instances of graphic discontinuity or mismatched temporal or spatial visual relations between shots are common, especially with material filmed from "real life." Instead of using editing techniques to join unified visuals, the teaching film employs them, in a utilitarian way, to separate illustrative material, with little regard for aesthetic relationships. For example, in a segment illustrating stem development in *Plant Growth* (Encyclopaedia Britannica Films, 1931), there is no conventional establishing shot to delineate the overall space and to show the spatial relations of the stem parts. Instead, a series of shots, all extreme close-ups in time-lapse photography, cut abruptly from a leaf pushing up through soil, to a single undulating stem, to a single tendril twining around a taut string, to several tendrils moving in the air. The graphic relationship between the shots is startlingly discontinuous and threatens to interrupt the viewer's flow of attention. The continuous narration holds the viewer's attention and its coherence allows the interpretation of discontinuous visual information. Within the lesson segments of the films, instances of aesthetically mismatched visuals are common, and the visual part of the film-lesson often becomes a series of unrelated filmic "events" cut to illustrate what is being described by the narrator. The films ignore the unifying potential of visual relationships that the film medium offers and use instead the content of the narration to provide continuity.

Unlike Hollywood style, which uses dissolves and fades to indicate temporal ellipses in the story flow, in teaching films fades and dissolves alert the viewer to a change in emphasis in the film. As described earlier in the discussion of form, teaching films set up a contrast between the introductory segment and the presentation of the lesson material. To emphasize the end of the introductory prologue and the beginning of the lesson material, the editing technique of the fade-out, fade-in is most often used. This stylistic technique reinforces the transition into the major part of the film and cues the viewer to pay closer attention to the real purpose of the film, the upcoming lesson content, than to the "emotional" cinematic appeals of the prologue. This technique reinforces the film's formal organization by emphasizing the contrast between the introductory prologue and the film's main lesson material.

Dissolves or fades are also sometimes used as stylistic techniques to indicate the separation of segments within the body of the lesson. For example, *The Dairy Industry* (Vocational Guidance Films, 1942) has seven segments—credits, prologue, description of the dairy farm, description of the job of the dairy farmer, demonstration of dairy plant operations, description of jobs in the dairy industry, and procedures for obtaining a job in the dairy industry. The technique of fade-out, fade-in is used in *The Dairy Industry* for the purpose of indicating the end of each segment and the beginning of the next; it directs the viewer's attention to the development and progression of the lesson material. However, this technique places so much emphasis on the separation of the segments that the film becomes a composite of discrete sequences with only the general dairy theme to unify them.

Even in later films that incorporate narrative, or story elements, into the lesson, the dissolve is used to cue the viewer to a change in film emphasis. For example, the lesson in *Electricity: How to Make a Circuit* (Encyclopaedia Britannica Films, 1959a) is designed within a frame story about two children who construct their own telegraph system. The story scenes alternate with sequences outside the story space—filmed lab demonstrations and animated sequences—that explain concepts of electricity. Dissolves, and the content of the narration, indicate the movement in and out of the story space—to the lab setting and the animated world and back to the story space. As a technique that is repeated throughout the film to reinforce the lesson, the dissolve is important in the formal development and becomes a motif in the film's style.

The traditional classroom lesson prescribes that students interact with lesson material and that the pace of the lesson be moderated to their learning needs. Because the viewer of the educational film has no opportunity to affect the pace of the lesson presentation for his or her understanding, the film must present its lesson material clearly and precisely. The uses of editing in the teaching film support this goal. Graphic material is cut to illustrate the factual content of the narration, and the techniques of fades and dissolves function to separate the film-lesson into clearly delineated segments and to cue the viewer's attention to changes in emphasis. These stylistic techniques allow lesson material to be presented with a degree of control and precision. The disunifying potential that they have on the film form is offset by the authoritative content of the audio narration.

Uses of Sound

In its use of sound, the teaching film is characteristically a film narrated by a single male voice of authority and includes no diegetic sound (i.e., sound motivated from within the film space). The stylistic element that functions most directly to support the form and intent of the teaching film is the voice-over narration. It is through the voice of the narrator that the content of the film's lesson is presented; all other elements in the film are motivated by his commentary. This is quite different from the situation in dramatic fiction films, where character traits and goals "cause" things to happen. In all the films I analyzed, the voice of the narrator is the single most unifying formal element. In films produced before the 1950s the voice of the narrator is the only sound on the audio track. No sounds originate from within the film, even when the visuals illustrate naturally noisy material. Except for the voice of the narrator, the films are silent films. In films produced later an occasional sound effect is included to give emphasis to a visual, but the voice of the narrator is never subordinated. Later films include music under the introductory and closing segments, which acts to separate them stylistically from the lesson segments and also becomes part of the preliminary rhetorical and stylistic attempt to motivate the viewer emotionally.

The voice of the narrator performs several functions. First, it directs the viewer's attention to material in the film. The narrator often refers to the visual material in the film through statements that direct and interpret, such as "watch what happens when we apply heat . . ." and "the nodding movement of the flower is caused by. . . ." Second, it acts as the major unifying element within the lesson content. Many of the films are so formally dependent on the content of the narration that a reading of the script alone provides much of the educational experience of the film. Even in films where demonstrations constitute a major part of the content, the narrator thoroughly describes the visual content and guides the viewer through the correct understanding of the material.

As a stylistic technique in the silent world of the teaching film's visuals, the effect of the single voice of the narrator is to sanction the visual material. Even though the visuals may be aesthetically unrelated and discontinuous, the unified content of the narration gives them legitimacy in the film style.

SUMMARY: THE LEARNING EXPERIENCE IN THE TEACHING FILM

Form and style in the teaching film construct a learning experience that is different from nonmediated lessons in several significant ways. In the teaching film the traditional lesson is compressed into three parts—prologue, presentation of lesson material, and conclusion—that exclude all teacher and student interaction with the lesson material. The preparatory steps of a traditional lesson are replaced by the brief prologue to the lesson topic that motivates viewing through emotional appeal. Because the preliminary interaction with subject material that is part of preparing students for new learning experiences is absent, learning in the film-lesson is isolated from, not connected to, previous learning experiences.

The pace of the traditional classroom lesson is adjusted as students and teacher interact with lesson material. One of the "essential principles . . . in lesson planning" is to "make provisions for individual [student] differences" (Strayer, Frasier, & Armentrout, 1936, p. 208). The teacher is directed to "abandon" the planned lesson material "whenever the class response indicates that certain points need to be cleared up" (p. 217). Film form is in conflict with these requirements, and the learning experience offered through the teaching film excludes the opportunity for teacher, student, and subject matter interaction. Instead, the teaching film determines the pace of the lesson and requires that viewers give close attention throughout its length. Through the use of editing and sound techniques the pace of the lesson information is brisk. No interruptions or questions from viewers are possible, and there is very little repetition. In its place, the teaching film offers an abundance of visual information supplied by special cinematographic techniques to support the lesson content in the narration. If a viewer does not understand a point, he or she must watch and listen closely in the hope that further content will offer clarification.

Student participation and application, an important step for enhancing learning in the classroom lesson, are replaced in the teaching film by vicarious experiences offered through demonstration techniques. One of these techniques is dramatization. The teaching film assumes the ability to generalize from film experience to concrete experience. For example, in the film *Reading Maps* (Encyclopaedia Britannica Films, 1955) the student must have the ability to understand how maps and map-making processes demonstrated by the two boys in the film can be applied to the real maps that he or she may encounter later. In addition, the teaching film requires that the viewer be able to differentiate between the film world created through technical methods and the "real" world. When the film demonstrates through animation or time-lapse photography, the information it provides is real but cannot be experienced outside the film medium by the viewer.

After the material of the film-lesson has been presented, the film ends with a brief recapitulation of the topic. The film-lesson is isolated from future lessons. One of the indications of a "good" traditional classroom lesson is that it provides "a real stimulus for study in preparation for the next day's work" (Strayer, Frasier, & Armentrout, 1936, p. 216). Even if the subject of the teaching film is part of the classroom curriculum, form in the film itself isolates the lesson experience through film conventions that require stylistic unity and closure. Techniques of closure such as a musical crescendo under the closing statement "and that's the story of the steam engine" give no indication to viewers that the lesson material of this film relates to any other future learning experience.

The learning experience in the teaching film is essentially a viewing experience. All "lessons" in the teaching film are visualized. A film is a system of audio and visual relationships, and the film medium provides stylistic techniques to direct the viewer's attention and create meaning through these relationships. The form of the teaching film organizes the content of the film-lesson precisely through the audio narration, but meaning in the film comes from the narration's relationship with the film's visual material. Therefore the lesson in the teaching film is limited by the technical ability of the film medium for representation. Even when the subject of the lesson does not seem appropriate for film demonstration, such as the topic of a balanced diet in *Magic Food* (General Pictures Productions, 1947), concepts are made concrete through visual representation, and the fundamentals of a balanced diet become a magician's props. The pupil of the film-lesson is a closely guided viewer in a concrete, visible world.

REFERENCES

Bordwell, D., Staiger, J., & Thompson, K. (1985). *The classical Hollywood cinema: Film style & mode of production to 1960*. New York: Columbia University Press.

Bordwell, D., & Thompson, K. (1986). *Film art: An introduction* (2nd ed.). New York: Knopf.

Coronet Films. (Producer). (1958). *Panama Canal* [Film].

Dodd, D. I. (1898). *Introduction to the Herbartian principles of teaching*. New York: Macmillan.

Ellsworth, E. (1987). Fiction as proof: Critical analysis of the form, style, and ideology of educational dramatization films. *Proceedings of selected research paper presentations at the 1987 AECT Convention sponsored by the Research and Theory Division*. Atlanta.

Encyclopaedia Britannica Films. (Producer). (1931). *Plant growth* [Film].

Encyclopaedia Britannica Films. (Producer). (1935). *The work of rivers* [Film].

Encyclopaedia Britannica Films. (Producer). (1943). *The elements of electric circuits* [Film].

Encyclopaedia Britannica Films. (Producer). (1949). *The ears and hearing* [Film].

Encyclopaedia Britannica Films. (Producer). (1955). *Reading maps* [Film].

Encyclopaedia Britannica Films. (Producer). (1959a). *Electricity: How to make a circuit* [Film].

Encyclopaedia Britannica Films. (Producer). (1959b). *Simple machines: The inclined plane family* [Film].

General Pictures Productions, Inc. (Producer). (1947). *Magic food* [Film].

Gramet, C. (1934). Making an educational movie. *The Educational Screen, 13* (1), 5–7.

Jonassen, D. H. (1984). The mediation of experience and educational technology: A philosophical analysis. *ECTJ, 32* (3), 153–168.

Sless, D. (1981). *Learning and visual communication.* New York: John Wiley.

Strayer, G. D., Frasier, G. W., & Armentrout, W. D. (1936). *Principles of teaching.* New York: American Book Co.

Vocational Guidance Films, Inc. (Producer), & Iowa State College Vocational Education (Associate Producer). (1942). *The dairy industry* [Film].

Wells, H. (1951). *Elementary science education in American public schools.* New York: McGraw-Hill.

Young America Films (Producer). (1944). *The steam engine* [Film].

3
Open–Ended Films, Dead–End Discussions: An Ideological Analysis of Trigger Films

MIMI ORNER

There is nothing natural or inevitable about what gets taught in schools. School subjects are all social constructions with specific histories. To quote Philip Corrigan,

> Learning any subject is learning a language. Learning a language is learning social relations; learning esteemed, approved and proper expressive forms; understanding obedience, respect, acceptability . . . *what it means to be Good.* What counts as a valid expressive form within schooling is thus intimately connected with, and strongly regulative of, our sense of our social identities. (Quoted in Livingstone, 1987, p. 30)

Official educational language and knowledge are experienced as Other by the majority of students. Most students do not relate to these language and knowledge codes through their own lived experiences of class, race, gender, and ethnicity. It is no easy task to learn the rules of "correct," "socially acceptable" behavior. Over the last 40 years, educational films have played a significant role in modelling so-called proper conduct. By investigating the hidden curriculum of educational films, it is possible to analyze some of the concrete modes through which official school knowledge is distributed in classrooms. A consideration of practices and assumptions regarding educational films and their use illuminates often-ignored relations between school life and structures of ideology, power, and economic resources in which schools are embedded.

An examination of the use in schools of what have come to be called trigger films can shed light on how the imperatives of dominant educational theory inform and transform certain tendencies of cinematic practice. Trigger films are short (usually no more than several minutes long), problem-centered, and designed to engage students in contemporary dilemmas. These films briefly present moral dramas and then suddenly stop, leaving viewers "triggered" to respond. In a characteristic trigger film from a series on reckless driving, a group of teenagers are shown provoking a teenage friend to drive faster. The situation is abruptly stopped in midstream, and the audience is expected to supply an ending. Proponents argue that, unlike other educational films on subjects such as reckless driving, trigger films make no effort

> to convey information or values. [Trigger] films don't warn about the consequences of reckless driving—no crunching of metal, no ambulances, no earsplitting sirens. By watching realistic situations with which he can identify, the young driver can project his own feelings, expectations and experiences into spontaneous group discussion, hopefully with a therapeutic effect. (Miller, 1971, p. 64)

Ideologies that make plausible the educational and therapeutic agendas of trigger films deserve serious consideration. Therefore, as background to my analysis of trigger films, I will describe their history, beginning with the educational milieu from which they arise. Then, I will address how the form, style, and mode of address of trigger films function to support the ideological goal of getting students to talk in educational settings. Finally, I will raise questions concerning the contexts in which these educational films are received.

EDUCATIONAL AGENDA

Traditional histories of the use of trigger films in education generally tie the production of these films to priorities in the areas of educational psychology and instructional design. Educational psychologists and technologists have attempted to correlate various types of learning with particular media. They claim that some methods of delivery are more appropriate and successful for dealing with "knowledge transfer" as opposed to "skill attainment." Learning, for these researchers, is thought to be divisible into three separate domains—the psychomotor, the cognitive, and the attitudinal or affective domain. The division of learning into three separate domains has significantly influenced educational film practice generally and the construction of trigger films specifically. Trigger films are a deliberate attempt at translating discourses of affective learning into filmic technique.

Often the objectives of affective learning are achieved through personal interaction with one's self and/or others. Many times such an instructional objective . . . will be to expand the learners' awareness by helping them to attain competency in recognizing and successfully coping with situations they are likely to encounter relative to their own feelings and with sensitivity to the feelings and viewpoints of others. The attainment of such a goal may be accomplished by a variety of methods such as on-site observations, discussions, role playing, and so forth; but, whatever the method, information must be introduced as the stimulus for the learners. This information might: provide specific perceptions, generate a particular mental state, dictate an emotional set, present a socially charged atmosphere, or offer a distinctive mood to any individual learner. . . . A trigger film is just such an external stimulus resource, designed to set-the-stage to generate and elicit responses to the situation and information provided. (Newren, 1974, p. 1)

The rationale behind trigger filmmaking is clearly linked to assumptions regarding the ability of films to elicit emotional responses and subsequently verbal responses from viewers. Advocates of trigger films take for granted behaviorist beliefs in cause–effect relationships. They assume that students are capable of being "triggered" by "stimuli." In addition, classrooms are unproblematically viewed as appropriate sites in which students can discuss controversial topics. There is a serious lack of attention paid to social, political, and economic differences and power relations that delimit the readings and speakings students are able to produce in specific classrooms at particular historical moments. That some students may have a great deal of experience with the "dilemmas" presented in the films is also not acknowledged. Instead, students are regarded simultaneously as an undifferentiated mass and as autonomous individuals. In both cases, important social differences between and among students based on gender, physical ability, race, sexuality, class, religion, size, geographic region, and ethnicity are ignored. And because students' identities, subjectivities, and social positions are ignored, discourses of affective learning conceive of students as needing and responding to the same "stimulus." All students are seen as lacking the same skills and in need of "expanded awareness" and "competency in coping with situations regarding their own feelings and the feelings and viewpoints of others." Furthermore, teachers and other educational professionals are positioned as people who have dealt conclusively and successfully with their own implication and involvement in the controversial topics under discussion. Teachers and other educators involved in affective learning are assumed to practice the "correct responses" and "proper behavior" the films are encouraged to "trigger."

HISTORICAL DEVELOPMENT

Mainstream histories locate the source of the idea for the trigger film as the brief films produced by Seat-Cohen, a French psychologist. Seat-Cohen's films contained mysterious situations and images similar to those of the Rorchach and Thematic Apperception tests. Similarly, interpretations of these films were linked to individualized viewers who could be led by the films into self-analysis. Alfred Slote, Assistant Director of the University of Michigan Television Center, transformed Seat-Cohn's ideas and created the trigger film format. Slote, who is credited with coining the term "trigger," has been active in the development of this technique for teaching purposes.

> The meaning of the term, "trigger," as applied to this film format and technique, is that the film acts as a catalyst by presenting in a crystal clear segment of time, a myriad of selected—but often ambiguous—details, concerned with a provocative topic, all of which are designed and calculated to evoke, or "trigger," viewer response. (Newren, 1974, p. 2)

Precursors of the trigger film format include a series of discussion-generating films entitled Pre-Retirement Education, developed by Slote and the University of Michigan Department of Gerontology and produced by the National Film Board of Canada and the U.S. Air Force. The "new concept in film" (Miller, 1968, p. 876) emerged in the late 1960s with the production of a trigger film series prompted by research indicating a need to change young drivers' attitudes and behaviors. After conducting a survey of 288 unmarried male drivers aged 16 to 24, a team of researchers at the University of Michigan (Donald C. Pelz, Stanley H. Schuman, Nathaniel J. Ehrlich, and Melvin L. Selzer) concluded that

> multiple and complex factors operate in the young driver . . . and emotional factors involving use of the automobile as an expressive instrument are important in accidents and particularly in moving violations. This phenomenon is more characteristic of those who stopped their education at high school than of those who went to college. (Miller, 1968, p. 876).

Examining the ideological positions underlying the methodologies and conclusions of research that supports trigger films helps contextualize the priorities and modes of address of the films themselves, particularly in relation to race, class, and gender differences. The remark made by the survey researchers regarding college education reveals a disturbing elitism. Moreover, the data gathered are used to generalize about all young drivers, when only males were surveyed. Perhaps unsurprisingly, in the trigger films that resulted from this research, the young drivers with whom viewers are supposed to identify are virtually all white, middle class, and male. The assumption that the same "stimulus" can "trigger" all students presumes that all will be able to identify with the white, middle-class males depicted in the films, and that the situations these young men find themselves in are universal, that is, likely to happen to young women and men of color, poor and working-class students, and so on. The construction of a white, male, middle-class norm is certainly not a new development in the history of curriculum. What is unusual in the case of trigger films is the extent to which the films are premised on the expectation that students can and will identify with the characters. In their effort to "relate to hard-to-reach drivers who were high school seniors," the creators of the Trigger Films for Young Drivers series sought to

> evoke analysis and thoughtful speculation of dangerous driving situations among an age group of drivers who had already received driver education training, possessed operator's licenses, and who, in many cases, were suspected of being self-reliant to the point of complacency. . . . [The films] were developed to show behind-the-wheel behavior which would appeal and be corollary to a young driver's actual and fantasized experiences. (Newren, 1974, p. 3)

The titles of these films are short, ambiguous words or phrases that seem designed to operate as triggers on their own: *The Blonde; Go!; Homework; Party; The Key; Dreamer; Speed; Ponytail; The Date; Stop Sign; Lovebirds; Intersection; Tailgater; Don't Speed Up!; Afternoon Drive; Sandwich; Navigating; Yellow Light; C'mon, Get Going!; Hog;* and *Passing #1, #2,* and *#3.* Some of these, such as *The Blonde,* recall problematic attitudes and assumptions regarding women. An article designed to promote the acceptance and use of trigger films for affective learning contains the following stream-of-consciousness description of this film:

> So he's driving alone, driving along and he likes driving and he's a good driver and handles a car like he was born to handle a car not hunched up like a man who's learned late in life and he keeps a safe distance behind the car in front of him when this blonde in this convertible and with this pony tail bouncing along behind her passes him, shoots by him, giving him some exhaust and he thinks whee . . . whee . . . and lets her go but next thing she's slowed down and he sees her in her mirror and she sees him and they both grin and he takes off to pass her . . . with a honk of a horn and a shot of exhaust and a grin he takes off to pass her . . . and it's fun fun and full of

good feelings because they both know how to handle cars and they're both young with young bodies. (Miller, 1968, p. 876)

As I read this description, I am reminded of the stories that fill the pages of teen magazines such as *True Love,* where white, heterosexual, male dominance is equated with "good, clean, all-American fun." Proponents of trigger films take for granted that all teenagers relate to the kind of reckless driving portrayed in *The Blonde.* Much is made by trigger film producers of the differences between triggers and more conventional films on reckless driving in which white male narrators lecture on safety or gruesome accidents are displayed. The trigger film approach to reckless driving may look very different from these conventional films and it attempts to invite involvement and participation in characters' lives in ways quite unlike conventional films. But the audience that reckless driving triggers are constructed to appeal to is the same audience envisioned by the conventional films. All three formats overwhelmingly define and depict drivers as white, male, middle class, most often suburban, and presumably heterosexual. Reckless driving is then defined and discussed narrowly in terms of the imagined social realities of this group. For other groups in this culture, the meanings and realities associated with driving are very different. Some women, for example, may not see reckless driving as something they need to be cautioned against. I know several women who were so horrified by films portraying accidents involving cars and trucks that they refused to drive on highways for years after receiving their licenses. Other social, political, and economic issues concerning driving might be much more salient for groups marginalized by these films. But advocates of trigger films regard the social realities portrayed in the films as being somehow universal and applicable to all students' lives.

> The situations presented are slices of life, conflicts and problems faced by youngsters every day. . . . [For example,] *Homework* opens with a boy polishing a car, lovingly, thoroughly. His father looms up, belligerent, sarcastic. "Well, . . . have you done your homework yet?" Tempers flare, they argue, the boy flings himself into the car and speeds down the quiet street. Quick cuts (in black and white as well as in color) review the pieces of the flare-up, reveal the boy's emotional turmoil as he races away. (Miller, 1968, p. 878)

As in *The Blonde, Homework* depicts white, middle-class teenagers living on quiet, suburban streets, with sufficient economic resources to own their own cars. Viewers are construed as willing and able to identify with these socially isolated characters, who are portrayed out of context, with no sense of history or of even the existence of marginalized identities or group struggles. These triggers and the next series, on drug use, have much in common with other educational films when it comes to the extreme individualization of complex social problems. In the "drug triggers," social conflicts and power dynamics in society and in the lives of students are recast solely in terms of parent–child or intergenerational conflict. Drug triggers ask junior high school students to "seek answers from within relative to the personal temptations often associated with drug experimentation or use" (Newren, 1974, p. 3). There is no sense of the larger network of social, economic, and political relations involving race, class, gender, age, sexuality, and so on in which drug use is embedded.

Following discussions with a group of 12 teenage drug users on proposed themes and film techniques, trigger film producers began work in the spring of 1970 on a new drug series. The results—*Linda, The Window,* and *The Door*—are drug triggers "constructed around the themes of rebellion against authority, feelings of loneliness or boredom and conformity or status brought about by peer pressure" (Newren, 1974, p. 3). According to proponents, these drug triggers differ markedly from other drug education materials previously available. Stanley Schuman writes,

> [The] stereotypes . . . are so well known that students today routinely expect to see a melodramatic needle sequence or to hear an ex-addict's warnings. The ear-pounding emphasis is on facts (pharmacological, clinical, legal, etc.) with a strong element of fear, or on fear (death, disfiguration) with an element of fact. . . . Can we afford to ignore the subtlety and pervasiveness of drug abuse in an everyday context? (Quoted in Miller, 1971, p. 64)

One of the three drug triggers, *The Door,* has particular significance for me because I saw it in health class as a high school freshman. Unfortunately, I do not remember the discussion following the film—or indeed, whether there was one. Miller (1971) provides the following description of the film:

> The setting is a teenage party within a party, whose focal point is a bright red door behind which something is going on. Some of the guests are invited behind the door, others are excluded, and a boy playing chess observes the action and wonders about himself. There is no dialogue, only the music of the party. Young viewers can't help but add their own thoughts and experiences to a group discussion after watching this provocative film. (p. 65)

Several more series followed the production of these drug triggers at the University of Michigan Television Center. One series produced in

1971 deals with the insensitivity on the part of young people toward the needs of the elderly. "Aging triggers," according to the producers, "portray the reactions of elderly persons to differing monetary situations that confront them" (Newren, 1974, p. 4). Titles of these triggers include *To Market, To Market; Mrs. P; The Center; Dinner Time;* and *Tagged.* Also in 1971, a series of "mental retardation and the law triggers" were produced for use in the education of judges at conferences. These trigger films are curiously entitled *Jerry, Raymond,* and *Leonard.* Designed for adults, this set of triggers and two others, known as "dental triggers" and "secretarial triggers," vary from earlier productions in that "they are more clinical in nature, their intent being to provide information through the use of dialogue" (Newren, 1974, p. 5).

IDEOLOGICAL ANALYSIS

The specific ideological work attempted by trigger films deserves serious scrutiny. As an educational film form, triggers raise questions not only of cinematic practice but also of the impact of pedagogical theories on film making. How trigger films have been constructed to elicit a particular type of audience involvement relates both to the text/context problematic raised by many theorists in cultural studies and to the analysis of the hidden curriculum currently going on within education. The lack of endings in trigger films plays a big role in the hidden curriculum of these films, which attempt to get students to invest in the controversy presented and to talk in officially acceptable ways about the issues raised. The lack of narrative closure gives the illusion that trigger films are open-ended. They seem to generate meanings that are less fixed and limited. Instead of overtly advancing arguments, trigger films, producers argue, observe situations and events. But these events are heavily prejudged by the form and style of the films themselves. Even though the illusion of being able to discuss and choose from many alternative endings is maintained by the lack of an ending, it is clear that there are still negative connotations placed on many of the alternatives.

In the film *The Buddies,* the inflection and tone of voice of one of the young male characters come across as manipulative, as he tries to convince the innocent-sounding character to take a drink from the bottle of wine he is holding. Through the performance of the dialogue, viewers get the message from this film that it is not okay to drink. *The Buddies* ends with a freeze frame, signifying a moment of choice. Yet the film itself offers no choice—it is clearly loaded against taking a drink. Although students are supposed to be able to debate alternative endings for these films, it is obvious that some endings are totally inappropriate given not only the text, but the context of viewing as well.

Questions concerning the context in which a trigger film is screened cannot be ignored. What constitutes an appropriate ending for a trigger film is not determined by the text alone. In *The Buddies*, the institutional dynamics and constraints of the school and the relations within the classroom are stacked against any ending offered by students that goes against official school-knowledge codes of proper behavior. Teacher–student dynamics, the institutional space, lighting, seating arrangement, inability to leave the room without permission, and a myriad of other regulations and rules guiding behavior affect what can and cannot be said about trigger films. As David Morley (1980) asserts,

> The meaning produced by the encounter of text and subject cannot be read off straight from its "textual characteristics" or its discursive strategies. We need also to take into account what Neale [1975, pp. 39–40] describes as "the use to which a particular text is put, its function within a particular conjuncture, in particular institutional spaces, and in relation to particular audiences." (pp. 170–171)

As with other kinds of dominant educational media practice, trigger films conceive of students as more or less passive recipients of "preconstructed meanings already present in the text" (Kuhn, 1982, p. 157). However, unlike other kinds of educational media, the very rationale for the specific form and style of trigger films acknowledges active audience participation in their construction of knowledge. Quite literally, trigger films require audiences to finish the text. But as I have shown, the terms and direction of that "finishing" are severely constrained.

In examining further how this participation is constrained, I will focus briefly on the culture of the classroom and the nature of classroom discussions, speech, and silence. Ira Shor (1980) notes that working people and students "talk a lot among themselves, but grow quiet in the presence of authorities. To talk a lot in an institution, at work, at school, or in front of superiors is to be guilty of collaborating with the enemy" (p. 72). In the quote, Shor is not trying to say that teachers are the enemy, but rather that student "talk" is always enmeshed in an array of power relations that exist inside as well as outside the classroom. The student whose "talk" in a classroom is too enthusiastic may be thought of as a teacher's pet; the one whose talk is too rebellious may be seen as a troublemaker.

> Because a power struggle surrounds the use of words in every institution of life, there are tense rules and high prices to pay for talking. At the very least,

supervisors discourage people talking to each other because it interferes with productivity; in school, teachers dissuade students from talking to each other, or out of turn, not only to maintain order but also to maintain the teacher as the sole regulator of the talking. (Shor, 1980, p. 72)

Silence in the classroom can have many meanings. It can be seen both as a form of defense and as a form of resistance. Refusing to talk, according to Shor (1980), can prevent others (both teachers and students) from

knowing what you think or feel, and using it against you. It also sabotages a controlling process that needs your verbal collaboration. In a culture where superiors regularly humiliate subordinates, it becomes understandable for students . . . to stay self-protectively silent in class. (p. 73)

Curriculums like trigger films attempt to break the silence of students. But this is not done to create a classroom space where students can articulate what is meaningful to them. Rather, trigger films attempt to break the culture of silence so that presumably "passive individuals" can be made to actively engage with provocative topics within the terms set by the films' form and style, and within those set by the institution and the specific classroom teacher. Student talk following the screening of a trigger film can be regulated, judged, and disciplined. Student talk can also be a forum for students to display their familiarity with the codes and rules of "socially acceptable" behavior—whether or not they believe what they are saying. As Shor (1980) has observed, "talking a lot in class means commitment to the process" (p. 73). Talking, as far as advocates of trigger films are concerned, signifies a willingness to take up the positions overtly and covertly offered in the films. The measure of success for trigger films is their ability to elicit talk.

How the form and style of trigger films are utilized for provoking "socially acceptable" talk is significant. Two major strategies are used by triggers for this purpose. The first strategy, as already discussed, involves the withholding of an ending. The second strategy involves the ways in which spectators are invited to feel that they have an investment in the issues, that is, through the use of subjective camera angles, zooms, and shot scales, conventions borrowed from classic narrative cinema that connote a first-person point of view on the situation or dilemma.

The offer to viewers to invest in the issues presented in trigger films reveals an important layer of the ideological functioning of these films. Through the first-person point of view, spectators are asked to assume the position of the characters. But characters' positions are constructions enmeshed in ideologies of "socially acceptable behavior," ideologies of affective learning and official educational knowledge that are, as I stated earlier, experienced as Other by most students. Thus the invitation to invest in the issues of these films through the use of a subjective point of view serves to make the place of the Other appear to be the students' own, for the purpose of getting the students to speak. In other words, if students want or are able to invest in the issues presented in trigger films, then school knowledge is no longer Other. And if school knowledge can be presented as if it is no longer Other, then the resistance to speak is undermined.

To Market, To Market, a film from the series of "aging triggers," follows "a proud but vulnerable elderly lady doing her meager marketing and then having to present her food stamps to an insensitive cashier" (Miller, 1971, p. 66). A number of formal and stylistic elements function to try to get viewers into the action. High angle shots, canted angles, and slow zooms imply a mental state or point of view. These camera techniques contribute to a sense of victimization that surrounds the central character. The older woman in the film is made to appear trapped in a world of insensitive and rude teenagers. In the close-up shots of her face, she seems to be pleading with viewers to sympathize with her situation. Spectators are asked to identify with the world of the older woman when the camera stays focused on her after her run-in with a teenager at the meat counter. These optically subjective techniques, which attempt to get viewers into the dilemma, culminate in the final shot of the film—a freeze frame that carries connotations of a highly significant situation or moment of choice. The lingering freeze frame of the woman's face at the end of this film adds to the illusion that what is asked of spectators is their own freely given solutions; in fact, however, the form and style of *To Market, To Market* have already actively constructed a stance toward the dilemma. We are not encouraged through the form and style of this film to identify with the rude and insensitive teenagers. Nor are we invited to question why the woman has food stamps. We are encouraged to sympathize with the older woman and to understand the issue or dilemma as one of rude teenagers. However, the sense that a given viewer makes of this—or any—film depends as much upon the viewer's social positioning and the historical and social context of reception as on the text itself.

The centralized production of trigger films, like that of other educational media, means that the same film is shown to thousands, even millions, of students around the country, regardless of social, cultural, political, and economic differences. Although trigger films are premised on the belief.that student viewers will identify with the situations and characters presented, what is portrayed in the films in fact reflects particular cultural values, languages, and lifestyles that may be far removed from the experiences of students and teachers in specific classroom settings. Trigger films are not viewed by a uniformly receptive population; instead, they are accepted, rejected, renegotiated, and transformed by students and teachers positioned socially and politically according to race, class, gender, sexuality, ethnicity, region, size, age, physical ability, and so forth.

Many educators argue that the use of prepackaged, ready-made media infringes on the personalized, local nature of their classrooms, an objection that applies not just to the media texts themselves, but also to the instruction manuals teachers often receive when using centrally produced media. Teacher guides and discussion materials do more than merely offer suggestions for how to use the film or video text. These "support" services attempt to persuade teachers to take on the values of the professional designer or "educational expert." The following advice is intended for users of trigger films:

> When conducting a trigger discussion or experience, the leader should facilitate, rather than direct, the process. The following are two basic guidelines for discussion facilitators:
>> Listen carefully—often a moment or two of attentive silence will be necessary to "break-the-ice," prod audience response, and/or stimulate brisk interactive discussion.
>> Interact judiciously—use initiating questions to approach topics for possible discussion; responsive questions might be asked to acknowledge or clarify a discussant's reply or bring forth an elaboration; also, repeating or echoing a response is a good technique for building rapport with the audience, stimulating extended discussion of a point, and for focusing group attention on an expressed observation or feeling.
>
> The facilitator's role is a difficult one. The stage is set for self-discovery when the group understands the purpose for their gathering and when they actively participate. The facilitator must strive to have the audience express what *they* think and feel. Facilitator–audience interaction should be kept to a minimum, with the emphasis being placed on audience–audience interactive participation. In this give-and-take type atmosphere . . . one must be patient and not attempt to force discussion. One must avoid value and moral judgements or views—allowing the audience to arrive at its own conclusions. This is generally achieved by being neutral—neither accepting nor disapproving—but encouraging and supporting the participants views—being interested in replies. (Newren, 1974, p. 10)

The focus in these guidelines for discussion on nondirective, self-discovery, experience-based curriculums clearly fits into an educational project attempting to respond to the demands put forth in the late 1960s for relevant curriculums. Trigger films and the discussions they are designed to provoke must be understood in this context. But it is also important to note that the films discussed here are not just relics of the 1970s. These films cover a wide range of topics and are still being produced in the hopes of "breaking down people's defense mechanisms" (Miller, 1968, p. 878).

In addition to their avowed intent, a host of assumptions underlying the design of trigger films must also be taken into account. Their use as curricular materials raises many important pedagogical questions—the purpose of education, the content and form of the curriculum, and the nature of learning and teaching—as well as a number of issues relating specifically to cinematic practice: questions of re-presentation, mode of address, film form and style, narrative closure, and the social, political, and historical context surrounding interpretive activities. All of these are central to understanding the ideologies of these and other educational films. Additionally, as films designed specifically to be used as "stimuli" for "affective learning," trigger films reveal interconnections between dominant educational theory and aspects of mainstream cinematic practice.

Investigators of the hidden curriculum in education need to focus greater attention on film and television designed for use in classrooms. Those groups with access to the means of producing film and television programming for use in schools have tremendous power to depict what counts as valid knowledge and to determine who possesses it. Centrally produced, "professionally designed" educational television and film can contribute to the marginalization of students who already experience official educational language and knowledge as Other. Examining trigger films and the "talk" they are designed to provoke in classrooms provides insight into the ways in which some behaviors, understandings, and knowledge from within the collective culture become manifest in schools as that which is proper, moral, and objective.

REFERENCES

Kuhn, A. (1982). *Women's pictures: Feminism and cinema.* London: Routledge & Kegan Paul.

Livingstone, D. (1987). *Critical pedagogy and cultural power.* South Hadley, MA: Bergin & Garvey.

Miller, E. (1968). The trigger film triggers a response. *Audiovisual Instruction, 13* (10), 876–878.

Miller E. (1971). Trigger filmmaking. *Audiovisual Instruction, 16* (5), 64–67.

Morley, D. (1980). Texts, readers, subjects. In S. Hall, D. Hobson, A. Lowe, & P. Willis (Eds.), *Culture, media, language* (pp. 163–173). London: Hutchinson.

Neale, S. (1975). Propaganda. *Screen, 16* (2), 39–40.

Newren, E. (1974, March). *The trigger film: Its history, production, and utilization.* Paper presented at the annual meeting of the Association for Educational Communications and Technology, Atlantic City, NJ.

Shor, I. (1980). *Critical teaching and everyday life.* Boston: South End Press.

4
Producing Sponsored Films on Menstruation: The Struggle over Meaning

MARGOT KENNARD

Since the late 1940s, teachers and school nurses across the country have relied on films to teach young adolescent women about menstruation. In 1947, the Kimberly-Clark Corporation hired Walt Disney to make the first of these educational films, *The Story of Menstruation*. In the 40 years since that film was released, corporations manufacturing menstrual products have been the primary source of films to provide menstrual education in the school curriculum. Within the past five years alone, four corporations have sponsored new films, competing with each other for the same audience of pre-teenage girls.[1] Sponsoring corporations enjoy little competition from noncommercial producers of menstrual films. Presently, school nurses report that only one noncommercially produced film, *Dear Diary* (Franco & Shepard, 1982), is used regularly in some schools.[2]

The significant and often central role sponsored films play in current menstrual education practices makes the question of what and whose meanings are privileged in these films particularly crucial. I begin my exploration into this question by looking at what is meant by "sponsored film." Although sponsored films have received little attention from researchers in the fields of educational media and film studies, there seems to be general agreement on what defines a sponsored film (Perkins, 1982). A sponsored film is one whose costs, including those of production, promotion, and distribution, are all paid for by a business or organization. Many sponsored films are targeted for use in schools, where they are either loaned free of charge or purchased at a substantially reduced cost. For public schools operating on tight budgets, using a sponsored film over a nonsponsored film can amount to considerable savings.

Embedded in the definition of sponsorship is an assumption about the role of the sponsor as a decision maker occupying a particular position in a hierarchy of control. In what appears to be the only book in which the sponsored film is specifically addressed, the author Walter Klein (1976) writes, "A sponsored film is a motion picture, in any form, paid for by anyone controlling its contents" (p. xii). Klein, a well-known producer of sponsored films, accepts that "the producer's control is transcended by the sponsor's" (p. xii). In this chapter I will challenge this commonsense meaning of sponsorship and will demonstrate that the sponsor's attempt to control which meanings will be privileged in a film through content, form, and style of presentation is highly complex and always contested. To do this, I will focus on the process of producing sponsored films on menstruation.

THE CONTENT OF SPONSORED FILMS ON MENSTRUATION

Since the emergence of the Women's Health Movement in the early 1970s, a number of feminist scholars have investigated the cultural construction of menstruation (Delaney, Lupton, & Toth, 1988; Lander, 1988; Weideger, 1976). However, menstrual education, particularly as it has been practiced in schools, has largely been ignored. It appears that a study by Whisnant, Brett, and Zegans (1975) is the only one in the menarche or menstruation literature to analyze and critique the content of classroom materials most commonly chosen for menstrual education— commercially sponsored films and accompanying student booklets.

For their study, Whisnant et al. selected two widely used films, *The Story of Menstruation* (Kimberly-Clark, 1947) and *Naturally . . . A Girl* (Personal Products, 1973). In addition, they examined student booklets published by the corporations, including those that accompanied the two films in their study. Claiming that the booklets and films are "remarkably similar in information offered, orientation and philosophy, and format and appearance" (p. 816), Whisnant et al.'s study does not distinguish among the individual booklets or films. A close examination of the contents of these materials led those authors to conclude the following:

> The major concern of these [sponsoring] companies is with selling a product. Any educational endeavor they engage in must support their commercial interests. Their failure lies in their concern with avoiding controversial and unpleasant topics in communicating with potential consumers. (p. 819)

In their study, Whisnant et al. are critical of the omission of "unpleasant topics" such as menstrual discomfort like cramps and mood changes, the messiness, or any "graphic sense of what menstruating is like." According to Whisnant et al., the companies omit this content in their films and booklets because it "might provoke negative emotions in the young readers [viewers] who are potential consumers of their products" (p. 818). Absent from the materials is also "controversial" information on topics such as hormones and their effects on physiological and emotional functions such as increased sexual interest and activity. Although the materials discuss the internal reproductive organs in great detail, there is no mention of the external organs such as the clitoris or vulva, or of the relationship between internal or external organs.

Rather than presenting the experience of menstruation, Whisnant et al. found the films and booklets focus on menstruation as a "hygienic crisis" emphasizing sanitation, daintiness, and concealment. The researchers claim this representation of menstruation supports the commercial interests of the companies sponsoring these materials. Whisnant et al. explain that "the sanitary product becomes a substitute object onto which the problems of menarche and adolescence can be displaced, and mastery of the use of sanitary products gives an illusion of control over the body" (p. 818).

A CULTURAL STUDIES FRAMEWORK

I would argue that while Whisnant et al.'s pioneering study should be recognized for its attempt to address the relationship between economic interests and the construction of a particular menstrual education discourse, it implies a static view of the production of meaning. Recent work in cultural studies, specifically work by feminists, has begun to challenge a simplistic view of the construction of meaning that places powerful groups, such as corporations who sponsor films on menstruation, solely in "control" of the process of producing meaning. As Fraser (1987) points out, this view of who "controls" meaning supports a top-down notion of power that obscures the active side of producing meaning. Fraser believes that an important goal of feminist research is to demonstrate how women actively construct, deconstruct, and reconstruct social meanings (p. 116).

In the analysis that follows, I will profile the "active side" of constructing meanings as it occurred in the production of two sponsored films on menstruation: *Julie's Story* (Kimberly-Clark, 1983) and *Growing Up on Broadway* (Personal Products, 1984). By drawing on a cultural studies approach for my framework, I will show how the production of these sponsored films was a site of struggle and negotiation in which the sponsor acted as one contestant among other groups, including film-makers, producers, and actresses.

By a cultural studies framework, I am referring to a theoretical approach that was developed in the 1970s at the Center for Contemporary Cultural Studies in England. The framework derives from elements of Marxism, semiotics, structuralism, and post-structuralism. This approach has been useful for addressing questions concerning the construction and circulation of meanings in film and television and their relationship to the unequal relations of power in Western societies.[3] The notion of *struggle over meaning*, as it is formulated within cultural studies, refers to the process by which powerful groups in the culture attempt to make meanings that serve their interests, appear natural, commonsensical, or given, while less powerful groups resist this process and try to win legitimacy for meanings that serve their interests (Fiske, 1987). Interviews I conducted with those involved in the production of *Julie's Story* and *Growing Up on Broadway* allow me to profile the terms and results of the struggle over meanings of menstrual education that were played out on the production site.

I refer to the production site of the sponsored film as a *contested terrain*, a field of struggle on which the different groups and individuals involved in the production of *Julie's Story* and *Growing Up on Broadway* are located. The notion of a contested terrain challenges the common-sense idea that powerful groups necessarily control meaning. Rather, on a terrain, powerful groups interact and negotiate with other groups (Fraser, 1987).

In my analysis I borrow another term from cultural studies, *differently oriented interests*, to address how the groups and individuals producing different meanings of menstrual education were oriented to each other on the contested terrain. The concept of differently oriented interests enables me to demonstrate that not all groups and individuals occupy the same strategic position on the terrain; some have access to institutional and/or cultural power, while others do not.[4]

In this chapter, I discuss examples from the film texts that illustrate how the sponsors' interests inflected the menstrual education discourse with particular meanings. But I will also show how these meanings were challenged by the filmmakers, actresses, scriptwriter, and producer with investments in different meanings of menstrual education. I discuss how these challenges resulted in unstable and contradictory moments in the film's content, form, and style of presentation. Such moments make visible the way in which the sponsor's "control" over meaning in the film is constrained by other players with competing interests.

ON THE TERRAIN OF PRODUCTION: *GROWING UP ON BROADWAY*

In 1983, Personal Products, a subsidiary of the Johnson and Johnson Corporation, hired two independent women filmmakers, referred to here as Nancy Stein and Rachel Fuller, to make a new menstruation film to replace the corporation's existing film, produced in 1973. Personal Products is the only corporation in the menstrual products industry to sponsor four educational films about menstruation over the last 30 years. These include *Molly Grows Up* (1953), *It's Wonderful Being a Girl* (1960), *Naturally . . . A Girl* (1973), and the film produced by Stein and Fuller, *Growing Up on Broadway*, released in 1984. Personal Products entered the menstrual education market in 1939 with the publication of the booklet, *What a Trained Nurse Wrote to Her Younger Sister.* For the past 50 years, Personal Products has actively worked to update its print materials, consisting of student booklets and worksheets, along with teacher's guidelines that accompany the films.

I obtained details of the production process of *Growing Up on Broadway* during interviews I conducted with Nancy Stein and Rachel Fuller in the summer of 1986 in New York City. Stein and Fuller, who are based in New York City, were recommended to Personal Products by the producer of *Sesame Street*. Before they were offered the job, the women were given $2,000 to put together a proposal for a film on menstruation. They were told that Personal Products would supply all the information for the film, but that they needed to come up with a context for the film, or as Stein called it, a "gimmick." Fuller and Stein submitted a proposal for a film that would feature a group of young actresses from the cast of the Broadway play *Annie*. Their idea was formulated as a result of interviews they conducted with pre-teen girls for another film they were producing. In these interviews, all the girls wanted to sing the same line from *Annie*, "the sun will come out . . . tomorrow." Stein and Fuller concluded that "Annie is a real hero for girls the way Superman is a hero for boys."

Using references to *Annie* for a film on menstruation served Fuller and Stein's investment in a particular meaning of menstrual education. They wanted to make a film that would provide viewers an opportunity to learn about menstruation by hearing young actresses who worked together in the cast of *Annie* talk about menstruation and their own experiences about getting their period for the first time. The filmmakers found that many of the actresses, who varied in ages from 9 to 17, went through puberty while they were in the play. Stein and Fuller wanted these actresses to talk about being told to leave the play because their bodies were changing and they were too tall to continue playing their "little girl" roles. In the film *Growing Up on Broadway,* one of the actresses explains

> The stage manager used to put the height marker up and every three months each of us had to stand next to the mark to see how much we had grown. If you topped the mark, sorry Charlie, one month's notice . . . you were out of a job. I thought I was all washed up at 14.

This quote also illustrates how these young women were invested in a meaning of menstruation that was based on their own "everyday life" experiences.

During my interviews with Stein and Fuller, I learned that the sponsor, Personal Products, was invested in a different meaning of menstrual education than the filmmakers and actresses. Fuller described the corporate discourse on menstrual education as "sugar-coated," where everything about menstruation is "neat and clean." Personal Products' investment in using the theme of *Annie* to convey a particular meaning of menstrual education is illustrated in the following quote from the company's promotional literature mailed to elementary schools:

> The excitement of the theatre . . . the reaction and honest enthusiasm of the girls . . . and reassuring information for every young viewer . . . that's what makes *Growing Up on Broadway* so compelling, so ideal for the classroom. A warm and candid view of young girls maturing on Broadway and loving it! (Personal Products, 1984)

The promotional literature included a letter from Susan Keithler, Manager of Public Relations at Personal Products, and the person from the corporation in charge of the production of *Growing Up on Broadway.* Keithler's letter, addressed "Dear Educator," describes the new film as "warm, friendly, and upbeat. In a manner evoking confidentiality and trust it helps teach, in a contemporary style, the facts, while putting to rest the myths and mysteries of menstruation."

This discussion of the differently oriented interests of the filmmakers and the sponsor highlights the investments each had in selecting the theme of *Annie* to provide the context for an educational film on menstruation. The filmmakers saw the use of *Annie* as an opportunity for a group of young women to share their own experiences of going through puberty and getting their period for the first time. They believed an audience of pre-teenage girls would readily identify with the actresses and thus find the film entertaining as well as relevant and informative. On the other hand, the sponsor saw *Annie* as an opportunity to present information on menstruation through "young girls maturing on Broadway and loving it!" thus serving its interest in associating the company name and consumer products with an upbeat viewing experience.

In the following section I look at how these differently oriented interests in meanings of menstrual education were actually played out on the contested terrain of the production of *Growing Up on Broadway.* I will attempt to delineate the terms of the struggles and negotiations as they occurred in the production of the film. I will argue that the menstrual education discourse represented in the film came from a site of struggle where the sponsor was positioned strategically in a more advantageous position than the filmmakers but, nevertheless, acted as one player, responding to and negotiating with other players on the terrain.

Growing Up on Broadway is 15 minutes long and divided evenly into three segments. The first segment in the film is an animated lesson in the physiology of menstruation. The second segment is a documentary of a group of young actresses sitting around backstage, talking with each other about getting their period for the first time, and sharing information about menstruation. The third segment is a demonstration of various menstrual products. When Fuller and Stein were hired, Personal Products provided them with scripts for the lesson on the physiology of menstruation and the demonstration of menstrual products. It was up to the filmmakers to develop a format for incorporating the *Annie* theme into the film.

REAL GIRLS TALK ABOUT REAL EXPERIENCES

For the second film segment, Fuller and Stein chose to use a documentary format because they wanted a film form that would allow, as Stein put it, "real girls to talk about their own real experiences." This segment of the film opens with a long shot of six young girls tap-dancing together on a stage. It appears to be a rehearsal, and the girls are casually dressed in leotards and tights. Soon they are joined by the teenage actress Shelly Bruce, who appears in all three film segments as a "hostess." In the introduction to the film, Bruce tells the viewers that she played the part of Annie in the Broadway production when she was 13 and now she is 17.

When she walks on the stage the other girls stop dancing and gather around her. Bruce addresses the camera directly and says, "I'd like you to meet some of my friends." Each girl introduces herself by giving her name and tells if she played the part of Annie in the Broadway production or the national touring company. This scene establishes the relationship of the girls in the group. One of the girls in the group says, "One of the greatest things about being in the show is we became close friends and it was easier to talk about things like this." "This" refers to menstruation and getting your period for the first time. The focus is on their common experience of acting in *Annie* and particularly of having to leave the show when they started to go through puberty. After this introduction the group sits down and for the rest of this segment the girls in the group talk to each other and not directly to the camera. Bruce begins the discussion by saying, "We all realized there were advantages to growing up and the first sign you're getting there is when you first start having your period."

The girls' discussion resembles a "consciousness-raising" discourse, a particular kind of group discussion associated with the Women's Movement that began during the late 1960s and early 1970s. Many of the early feminist documentary films made during this time used conventions borrowed from consciousness-raising groups: *Growing Up Female* (Reichert & Klein, 1971); *Janie's Janie* (Ashur, 1971); and *The Woman's Film* (Smith, Alaimo, & Sorin, 1971). Feminist film theorist Julie Lesage (1978) identifies the consciousness-raising group style as a potentially progressive film form. Lesage writes that many feminist documentaries "came out of the same ethos as the consciousness-raising groups and had the same goals" (p. 507). She says,

> The major political tool of the contemporary women's movement has been the consciousness raising group. It was the act of naming previously unarticulated knowledge, of seeing that knowledge as political and of understanding that the power of this knowledge was arrived at collectively. (p. 515)

The fact that the consciousness-raising segment occurs around the sharing of the common female experience of menstruation could be viewed as an example of what Lesage calls "naming the unnamed." Invested in a meaning of menstrual education that legitimates women's experience of menstruation as a source of knowledge, Fuller and Stein selected a film form that had the potential of validating a wide range of feelings and experiences, including those that are often "unnamed" in our culture, where openly discussing menstruation is considered taboo. This potential is demonstrated during the group discussion when one of the actresses talks about her feeling of embarrassment over not starting her period.

> You know, all of my friends, most of my friends, have gotten their period already. I'm one of the oldest kids in my grade so I feel kinda weird, you know . . . no one ever asks me . . . yet when we talk about it, I feel . . . you know, kind of embarrassed . . . sometimes.

Another time, the potential of the consciousness-raising form is demonstrated when one of the girls shares her experience of getting her period for the first time.

> When I started mine in June during the week of finals and I was staying with friends 'cause my parents were back East and these friends were adult friends of my parents. I didn't know who to talk to, so the first thing I did was pick up the phone and call my best friend and said 'help me get through this thing.'

Although these are two examples where the potential of the film form to validate women's experience is realized, there are very few other examples in the film. For the most part, the girls do not speak comfortably and openly. Rather, the group discussion appears constricted and tense.

PUSHING THE POSITIVE

According to Fuller and Stein, it was a real "battle" with the sponsor, Personal Products, to prevent the scene of the girls talking from being "totally scripted and controlled." The sponsor was "terrified" of what the girls in the group might say. Fuller and Stein explained that the sponsor is primarily interested in selling its menstrual products and this economic interest inflects the film with particular meanings. The sponsor wants its corporate image and consumer products to be associated with only "positive" images of menstruation. Stein said, "They almost want to say cramps are a figment of your imagination . . . or most people don't get them."

In the film, menstrual "problems" are barely touched on. For example, during the group discussion one of the girls asks, "Do you get moody?" Another girl responds, "Well, my mother tells me I get moody. I tell her 'I'm not moody' and she says, 'Yes you are.'" This comment meets a quick response by a third girl in the group, who says confidently,

> They tell you when you get your period you're going to get cramps, you're going to have oily hair, which isn't true because I don't get any of them. I don't get moody, I don't get cramps and if I do, I exercise and they disappear.

The previous statement illustrates how discussion of topics such as menstrual discomfort, painful cramps, and emotional changes or oily skin and hair is closed down or constructed as dealing with problems that have easy solutions. Because of its investment in associating its products with an "upbeat" view of menstruation, the sponsor responded to the documentary form by trying to limit and restrict its potential to legitimate a full range of feelings and experiences.

According to Stein, it was often the girls themselves that "clamped down" on discussing the "unpleasant" aspects of menstruating or any menstrual "problems," such as cramps or irregular periods. She suggested this may have occurred because the public relations director for the corporation was present during the shooting of the documentary segment. "There was said and unsaid approval and disapproval. The girls knew what they were supposed to do and they knew they were supposed to present a positive picture of menstruation without anyone saying it." The sponsor was also able to restrict the content of the discussion by having "unofficial knowledge" or misinformation edited out of the film, such as one of the girl's comments that menstruation wasn't really blood but "red eggs coming out."

On the contested terrain of the production of *Growing Up on Broadway*, the sponsor, the young actresses, and the filmmakers, all with differently oriented interests and different positions on the terrain, interacted with each other over which meanings of menstruation would be privileged in the film. One site of struggle was limiting the group discussion to only positive meanings of menstruation. As Fuller put it,

> The biggest irritation to us was the [sponsor's] pushing of the positive over the edge. We wanted to address fears more openly. Here they are touched on and passed on to something else and they are never really addressed and given legitimacy. In a way you feel you don't have a right to be afraid. Yeah, that it's silly to be afraid.

The process of producing meanings that serve the interests of the sponsor was not accomplished without challenge from the filmmakers and young actresses. This challenge resulted in a final product that was not under the control of the sponsor, but nevertheless bears the traces of the struggle over meaning. These traces appear as unstable and potentially disruptive moments in the film's text. For example, in the documentary segment, the youngest girl in the film, a 9-year-old African-American—the only person of color in the group—voices her fear of bleeding to death.

> I always thought it was scary. . . . My friend said her older sister had one . . . um . . . she said that . . . she said that her older sister had it . . . she thought she was dying or something. She was scared . . . she thought she was bleeding to death.

After she finishes, there is an awkward silence in the group. The camera pans the group to reveal the other young women looking uncomfortable. Finally someone asks, "Does it really make you feel weak if you lose blood?" Quickly another girl responds, "No, not really, you don't lose that much blood." Again the young actresses themselves close down the discussion by redirecting it to simple facts: "You don't lose much blood."

I did not ask Stein and Fuller why the remark about bleeding to death was left in the film—a remark that has the potential to undercut the sponsor's investment in a "sugar-coated," "upbeat" meaning of menstruation. However, I would speculate that the sponsor left the remark in the film because it was made by the only person of color in the group. In this instance the sponsor's need to win approval from schools by including racial diversity competed with its need to construct an upbeat and reassuring meaning of menstruation.

In this chapter, I have demonstrated that although the sponsor, Personal Products, was strategically in a more advantageous position than the filmmakers, the film *Growing Up on Broadway* contains moments that contradict the sponsor's interest in an "upbeat," noncontroversial meaning of menstrual education. I have argued that these unstable moments are the result of the efforts of the filmmakers and actresses to inflect the film with different meanings of menstrual education that serve their interests. In the next section, I profile the terms of the struggles over meaning in the production of another sponsored film on menstruation, *Julie's Story* (Kimberly-Clark, 1983). I will continue to support my argument that on the terrain of production, the sponsor, Kimberly-Clark, was not completely in control. Instead the sponsor negotiated with other groups with differently oriented interests in meanings of menstrual education. I will demonstrate that like the production of *Growing Up on Broadway*, the contestation on the terrain of production of *Julie's Story* resulted in unstable and contradictory moments in the film text.

ON THE TERRAIN OF PRODUCTION: *JULIE'S STORY*

In the early 1980s the Kimberly-Clark Corporation decided to update its 1947 classic educational film, *The Story of Menstruation*. The film had been actively circulated for over 25 years and, according to the sponsor, had been viewed by more than 100 million young women.

The Kimberly-Clark Corporation contracted with a media company based in Knoxville, Tennessee, to make a new menstruation film, *Julie's Story*. In this chapter I refer to the media company employee who was responsible for the film as the "producer," Faith Wold. The production of *Julie's Story* is somewhat different from *Growing Up on Broadway*, because Wold subcontracted with an independent film production company. This arrangement placed Wold in a "middle" position in the production process, where she participated in negotiations between the sponsor and the filmmaker and scriptwriter.

The following discussion is based on interviews I conducted with Faith Wold during the fall of 1988. In an interview, Wold explained that a major struggle in the production of *Julie's Story* occurred over the privileged position the medical discourse occupies in the film. According to Wold, the sponsor wanted "more medical detail" than Wold felt the young girls could take in. The sponsor believed that the film would be better accepted by the schools and educational community if menstrual education was constructed through a medical/scientific discourse. Wold, along with the scriptwriter, Bev Meyer, was interested in making a film for an audience of young women and wanted the information on menstruation to be not only accessible, but relevant to their contemporary needs. Wold's investment in a different meaning of menstrual education was supported by her pre-production work with focus groups, a research method commonly used in commercial marketing research. This technique involves bringing together a group of eight to ten people, in this case, young girls the same age as the target audience for the film. In the focus group, Wold engaged the girls in an open-ended discussion about what they thought a film about menstruation should address. She learned that girls who are 11 or 12 want to know things such as "When will I start?" "Why have my friends already started and I haven't?" "What are cramps?" "When you have your period does that mean you're pregnant?"

Wold challenged the sponsor's effort to privilege the medical discourse in *Julie's Story* because she was invested in a different meaning of menstruation, one that validated women's experience of menstruation as a source of knowledge. Wold explained her investment in this way: "Girls want the 'real basics.' They don't care about ovulation. They don't care about the eggs moving through cycles. They don't care about Fallopian tubes." Wold and Meyer, the scriptwriter, engaged in ongoing negotiations with the sponsor to produce a film that would serve their meaning of menstrual education. This contestation over differently oriented investments in different meanings of menstrual education resulted in a situation where, according to Wold, "we basically just went back and forth and back and forth." Wold would present the sponsor with a script, and the sponsor would request that more medical information be "plugged in." Wold found that by the time they added everything Kimberly-Clark wanted, the script had "a very stilted feel to it." She said,

So most of the dryness of the film I would say came from this back and forth where we would have every part to the place where we thought we were done and then we'd have to plug in more medical information. More and more medical information became a larger part of the film as we went along.

FRACTURING THE MEDICAL DISCOURSE

In *Julie's Story* menstrual education is embedded within a dramatic narrative format that invites the viewer to identify with the character of an 11-year-old girl as she copes with getting her period for the first time. The producer and the scriptwriter structured the film around Julie in an effort to personalize the experience of menarche because they were invested in a meaning of menstrual education that legitimates women's experience as a source of knowledge. This investment is also demonstrated in the way the film provides all menstrual knowledge through women who are nonmedical experts: the school dance coach, Julie's mother, and an older teenage sister. This allows menstrual information to be presented by those who have direct experience with the event. The main character, Julie, shares her feelings about what is happening to her with her best girlfriend, Tracy.

The differently oriented interests in different meanings of menstruation disrupt the stability of the film. The discourse legitimating women's experience of menstruation as a source of knowledge clashes with the expert knowledge of the medical discourse. For example, Julie and her girlfriend Tracy ask questions about menstruation in the everyday conversational language of young women. However, when the adult characters answer, rather than using their own experiences as women who menstruate, they end up delivering stilted medical explanations in the language of a textbook.

The following example from the film not only illustrates the way the film closes down and limits the discourse of experience, but also demonstrates the tension in the film as it tries to silence information on sexuality. This excerpt from the film implies that fertilization is an activity involving only an egg. The sponsor's need to privilege "accurate" medical knowledge competes with a need to win approval from schools, which regard explaining fertilization as too controversial for the elementary classroom. This tension results in an unstable moment in the film text where sexual reproduction is constructed as "immaculate conception."

MISS THOMAS: This [egg traveling to the uterus] takes about three or four days, and as the egg travels along the tube, the lining of the uterus grows thicker.

JULIE: Why?

MISS THOMAS: So that if the egg gets fertilized, which is the first step when a woman is going to have a baby, it would have a nice soft place to live while it grows.

TRACY: How big are the eggs?

MISS THOMAS: Very small. So small that they can only be seen with powerful microscopes.

JULIE: But what does that all have to do with my getting my period? I'm not going to have a baby, am I?

MISS THOMAS: Well, of course not, honey. You see when the egg isn't fertilized it dissolves and the lining of the uterus isn't needed so along with blood and fluid it is passed out of the body through the vagina. That's called menstruation. I know you girls call it your period but the proper medical word is menstruation. This flow usually lasts from three to seven days and then the whole cycle begins again.

The interview with Wold helped reveal the stakes the sponsor has in a noncontroversial meaning of menstrual education. She explained that for the sponsor, the main audience for the film is not young girls but the school board. According to Wold, the sponsor believes that "if you don't get the school board behind you then you don't get into a school." The sponsor protects the corporate image and its products from possible disapproval and criticism by privileging the medical discourse on menstruation and silencing sexuality. Wold elaborated on the sponsor's investment.

> Kimberly-Clark regards this film as their official presence in the schools. To them the film is Kimberly-Clark, and Kimberly-Clark is the film. And so the film has to embody everything that they believe as a corporation. It has to be a film that shows them to be a good corporate citizen, the kind who cares for you and your school district.

Another site of struggle in which the sponsor's economic interest clashed with Wold's interest in validating a range of women's experiences was played out over the construction of menstruation as a "positive" experience. Wold said, "They [the sponsor] don't even want to acknowledge cramps. They want menstruation to be really fun, something you want to happen all the time, not just once a month." The corporation is invested in this meaning because "they don't want their product to be associated with something that is viewed as scary or negative."

The following example illustrates how the sponsor attempted to inflect *Julie's Story* with a particular meaning of menstrual discomfort. Tracy asks her older sister, Beth, who is 18, "What about cramps? Didn't I see you in bed with a heating pad one day?" Beth responds, "Well, sometimes girls do have some discomfort, but there are a lot of ways to make yourself more comfortable, like using a heating pad." Tracy replies, "What a pain." And Beth answers, "Not really. And after all, it's worth it. Being a woman is something special."

Like many other moments in the film, this scene opens up the potential for a discourse of experience, with the expectation that Beth will share her own experience with menstrual cramps. Instead, the film closes down that opportunity when Beth answers the question by referring to "girls" and "women" in general rather than to herself. This example highlights how the continual opening up and closing down of a discourse validating women's experience as a source of knowledge threatens the stability of the film.

The research discussed in this chapter is important for two reasons. First it supports the claim that the process of producing sponsored films is played out on a contested terrain of struggle and negotiation. While the sponsor is located strategically in the most advantageous position on this terrain, groups on the margins, such as women filmmakers, scriptwriters, actresses, and producers, challenge the constraints of sponsored film production. The research demonstrates that these challenges created unstable moments in the menstrual education discourse produced in both *Growing Up on Broadway* and *Julie's Story.*

Second, the research discussed in this chapter sheds light on the investments sponsors have in privileging a particular discourse on menstrual education. For example, their economic interest in associating consumer products with positive meanings of menstruation results in an effort to construct any menstrual "problem" as a nonproblem. In addition, the corporate investment in winning acceptance from school boards results in a silencing of information on sexuality. While these efforts were challenged by the filmmakers, producers, scriptwriters, and actresses, these challenges did not fundamentally change the dominant meanings in the film. The task of producing a menstrual education discourse that can meet the differently oriented interests of young women students must be shared by groups such as school health educators and by feminists involved in women's health issues, along with school administrators and teachers. Hopefully the research in this chapter offers a starting point in this effort.

NOTES

1. Between 1983 and 1989, the following menstrual products corporations sponsored new menstrual education films: Kimberly-Clark sponsored *Julie's Story,* Personal Products sponsored *Growing Up on Broadway* (these two films are discussed in this chapter), the Tambrand Corporation sponsored *Who Am I Now?,* and Procter & Gamble sponsored *I Got It.*

2. For a detailed discussion on menstrual education produced in sponsored films see Kennard (1989).

3. For a detailed list of further readings on cultural studies at the Center for Contemporary Cultural Studies, see Fiske (1987), pp. 288–289.

4. For a discussion of "differently oriented interests" see D'Acci (1988).

REFERENCES

Ashur, G. (Producer). (1971). *Janie's Janie* [Film].

D'Acci, J. (1988). *Women, television: The case of Cagney and Lacey.* Unpublished doctoral dissertation, University of Wisconsin—Madison.

Delaney, J., Lupton, M. J., & Toth, E. (1988). *The curse: A cultural history of menstruation* (rev. ed.). Chicago: University of Illinois Press.

Fiske, J. (1987). British cultural studies and television. In R. Allen (Ed.), *Channels of discourse* (pp. 254–289). Chapel Hill: University of North Carolina Press.

Franco, D., & Shepard, D. (Producers). (1982). *Dear diary* [Film].

Fraser, N. (1987). Women, welfare and the politics of need interpretation. *Hypatia: Journal of Feminist Philosophy, 2,* 103–121.

Kennard, M. (1989). *The corporation in the classroom: The struggles over meanings of menstrual education in sponsored films, 1947–1983.* Unpublished doctoral dissertation, University of Wisconsin—Madison.

Kimberly-Clark. (Producer) (1947). *The story of menstruation* [Film].

Kimberly-Clark. (Producer) (1983). *Julie's story* [Film].

Klein, W. (1976). *The sponsored film.* New York: Hastings House.

Lander, L. (1988). *Images of bleeding: Menstruation as ideology.* New York: Orlando Press.

Lesage, J. (1978). The political aesthetics of the feminist documentary film. *Quarterly Review of Film Studies, 3,* 507–523.

Perkins, D. (1982). The sponsored film: A new dimension in American film research. *Historical Journal of Film, Radio and Television, 2,* 133–140.

Personal Products. (Producer) (1953). *Molly grows up* [Film].

Personal Products. (Producer) (1960). *It's wonderful being a girl* [Film].

Personal Products. (Producer) (1973). *Naturally . . . A girl* [Film].

Personal Products. (Producer) (1984). *Growing up on Broadway* [Film].

Reichert, J., & Klein, J. (Producers). (1972). *Growing up female* [Film].

Smith, J., Alaimo, L., & Sorin, E. (Producers). (1971). *The woman's film* [Film].

Weideger, P. (1976). *Menstruation and menopause: The physiology and psychology, the myth and the reality.* New York: Knopf.

Whisnant, L., Brett, E., & Zegans, L. (1975). Implicit messages concerning menstruation in commercial educational materials prepared for young girls. *American Journal of Psychiatry, 132,* 815–820.

5
Selection, Presentation, and Student Interpretation of an Educational Film on Teenage Pregnancy: A Critical Ethnographic Investigation

BONNIE K. TRUDELL

This chapter explores the use of an educational film on teenage pregnancy, linking ideological analysis with practice in a ninth-grade sexuality education classroom. My analysis draws upon several interconnected strands of critical scholarship on the role of schooling in shaping cultural values and perpetuating inequitable social relations (Apple, 1979, 1982; Bernstein, 1977; Bourdieu & Passeron, 1977; Bowles & Gintis, 1976). Although they disagree about the process by which this occurs, those engaged in this critical appraisal of education share a conviction that curricular content and form are not neutral. Instead, classroom knowledge is seen as selected from a larger pool of possible knowledge, with the selection likely to privilege the interests of most powerful social groups.

Furthermore, as ethnographic studies of education have demonstrated, the ideology of dominant groups is not mechanically imposed on passive subjects in the classroom (Everhart, 1983; Valli, 1983; Willis, 1977). Instead, teachers and students, who are themselves members of gender, racial, class, and other social groups, have the capacity to actively reinterpret, negotiate, and resist such ideology. Thus, school knowledge is seen as constructed in a day-to-day process that is dynamic, complex, subtle, and full of contradictions. Analyzing educational media in the context of this classroom process, which has been largely neglected by researchers in education technology and media studies, is the focus of this chapter.

METHODOLOGY

The film to be examined, *If You Want To Dance* (New Dimension Films, 1983a), was embedded in a four-week sexuality unit in a required ninth-grade health education class. The report presented here is one detail in a larger ethnographic investigation of the construction of school sexuality knowledge in a specific classroom (Trudell, 1988). I will discuss the presentation of educational media on teenage pregnancy within this wider curricular context, focusing on the following broad questions:

1. With what points of view about sexuality and gender relations does the film invite students to identify on the basis of its form, style, and classroom use?
2. What factors influence teacher selection and presentation of the film?
3. What are student classroom responses and interpretations of the film's points of view? Are these similar across social groupings?

The setting for the study was a midwestern city of about 175,000. The key aspects of the context—the school (comprehensive public high school of about 1,800 students), incorporation of sexuality education in a physical education department, and teacher (certified in both physical education and health, with 12 years teaching experience)—are similar to those in other U.S. contexts where school sexuality education is offered (Orr, 1982; Sonenstein & Pittman, 1984).

Data were obtained in 1985–86 by daily classroom observations, other school and district observations, and interviews of teacher and students. With specific regard to the film, data were collected during a half-day service meeting of district health teachers (at which they previewed and decided to show the film to students), ongoing formal and informal interviews with the classroom teacher, observations on the day the film was shown, a subsequent private screening for closer study, and open-ended interviews with 23 of 24 students (13 females and 10 males) who watched it. The latter explored student interpretation of the film's purpose and message and clarified the meaning of their classroom responses. Parent permissions were obtained for all student interviews; the community (Woodland), school (Van Buren), teacher (Mrs. Warren), and student names are all pseudonyms.

Just as I do not assume curriculum or educational media to be neutral, I do not view my selection of questions and events for closer scrutiny or interpretation as a neutral, objective process. Like others who reject the fact–value dichotomy of positivism, I believe that scientific neutrality is always problematic and never entirely value-free. Thus, my research, like the critical theoretical perspective from which it emerges, has a particular value stance and emancipatory purpose. That is, it "attempts to problematize what goes on in schools in terms of the reproduction of social inequality and the potential for social transformation" (Lather, 1986, p. 64). Simply put, I am committed to understanding the ways schooling perpetuates the unequal distribution of power and resources in our society and to changing these inequities. My research questions and analysis are an attempt to gain understandings that can inform action, especially classroom practice. As a white, 45-year-old, feminist, politically active, physically able, heterosexual, married mother with working-class roots, I do not offer this description and analysis as "objective," but as observations and conclusions that emerged from the theoretical framework and personal stance just delineated.

I shall begin by discussing my own interpretation of the film, focusing on points of view around sexuality and gender relations with which its content and form invite viewers to identify. Next I will briefly delineate the context of the classroom, including community, teacher, health course organization, students, and overall teaching strategies. Then I will describe the film's actual use in the classroom, including student classroom responses and considerations that influenced the classroom teacher's selection and presentation of the film. Finally, on the basis of student interviews, I will explore the students' interpretations of the film's purpose and meaning.

THE FILM

If You Want To Dance is a 14-minute color film produced for the U.S. Department of Health and Human Services by New Dimension Films (1983a). Its brevity, open-ended conclusion, and suggested discussion questions set up a context for intended use as a "trigger" film (see Orner, Chapter 3 of this volume). According to an accompanying brief discussion guide (New Dimension Films, 1983b), it is "Award Winning" and "designed to be used by schools, PTA's, community organizations and other groups concerned about teenage pregnancy and sexuality" (p. 1). The guide further states that "the film has been viewed and accepted by multiple religious and civic organizations as well as public and private agencies. Both young people and their parents feel the story is very realistic and has impact" (p. 1).

Given its government funding and these specific references to acceptability among adults involved in mainstream institutions, the film seems intended to reinforce rather than contest dominant social norms about adolescent sexuality. These will be subsequently discussed in greater detail.

The guide describes it as "appropriate for junior high and high school classes such as health, family life, parenting, counseling, etc." (p. 1), but suggests more specifically in a statement of purpose that males are a major target group: "One of the film's main objectives is to impress upon males that pregnancy is not just a girl's problem. Despite peer pressure, it is not fashionable to get a girl pregnant" (p. 1). Given its main characters and setting, it seems to be geared more specifically to white, middle-class, heterosexual, urban males.

The discussion guide offers the following brief synopsis of *If You Want To Dance*:

> The film begins with stark contrasts of scenes from a boys' physical education class and a hospital delivery room. The scene then switches to three high school boys talking in a locker room after a physical education class. Their discussion provides the audience with different views boys have about responsibility for teenage sexual behavior and possible pregnancy.
>
> The scene shifts back to a hospital room where two unwed teenage girls, Chris and Judy, are discussing pregnancy and the choices they have made in dealing with their babies. As they talk, they express some female views about sexual responsibility.
>
> In the final scene, while walking her baby in the hospital, Chris is visited by her boyfriend, Jeff. Jeff's two locker room friends arrive to see Chris and Jeff arguing about adoption and who was responsible for the pregnancy. Jeff storms out of the hospital, triggering a conversation between his two friends in which one remarks, "If you really care about a girl, you don't get her pregnant in the first place." (p. 1)

The film's form and content combine to portray stereotypical gender differences and a wide communication chasm between the sexes. With regard to form, these ideas are initially suggested by the rapid juxtaposition and "stark contrasts" between young men (Jeff and his friends) playing basketball while a young woman (Chris) delivers a baby. The camera covers the locker room scene from a longer range, encompassing clothes-changing activity and extraneous noise, and then moves in close on the hospital conversation between the two young mothers, underscoring its intimacy.

The three interpersonal exchanges depicted in the film (involving only males, only females, and both sexes) also emphasize gender stereotypes and suggest little possibility for communication across the sexes. Males engage in bantering locker room talk; females engage in earnest and personal conversation; males and females together argue. In the first scene, Jeff and his male buddies banter with each other in the locker room while his girlfriend is at the hospital giving birth. Jeff is portrayed as an insensitive and sexist young man who is neither physically nor emotionally involved in the delivery of his baby. He objectifies women with jokes about "scoring," sees them as primarily responsible for birth control, and implies that the pregnancy is Chris' fault. An apparently more sensitive friend suggests that guys could prevent pregnancy by using condoms; but later in the conversation, Jeff questions this friend's authority by saying, "Anybody you could get pregnant would be too ugly to find anyone else." As the three young men leave the locker room for the hospital, where Jeff will visit Chris, the third friend makes an admiring remark about Jeff to the more sensitive friend: "Man, he sure does have it together."

The scene then shifts to Chris in a hospital bed after giving birth; she is talking with another unmarried teenager (Judy), who has just had her second child. In contrast to the bantering locker room talk among buddies, the two young women introduce themselves and immediately begin an intimate conversation. They listen and respond empathetically to each other as they discuss their pregnancy/birth experiences. They also discuss their relationship with the baby's father (Judy confides that her boyfriend left when she got pregnant a second time) and their respective pregnancy decisions. Both agree that abortion is an unacceptable option; Judy says she is keeping her baby, and Chris says she is giving hers up for adoption, since it is "best for the baby." The nurse then brings in Judy's baby, and Chris asks to see hers. While Chris is holding the infant in her arms, the camera lingers for several seconds on a close-up of its face. Chris looks lovingly at the baby, and the film cuts to the last scene.

The only female/male communication depicted in the film occurs in this last scene, during which Jeff arrives at the hospital as Chris is wheeling the baby down the corridor in a bassinet. After ogling a passing nurse (a gesture visible enough to draw laughter from several students watching the film), Jeff meets Chris in the hospital corridor. He begins impersonally by saying, "They said you had it," and later remarks, "Hey, how come you're still so fat? Sure you had it already?" He shows no interest in the baby and, when Chris reveals her last-minute decision to keep it, becomes angry and shouts, "I've got my whole life ahead of me, and I'm not going to let it go down the tubes just because *you* got pregnant." Chris begins to cry and argues back tearfully, "It wasn't just me." The two continue the argument, with Jeff shouting and Chris crying, until a male security guard appears; Jeff is then moved firmly down the corridor, while the sobbing Chris is led gently in the opposite direction by a comforting female nurse.

The film closes with a brief exchange between Jeff's two friends, who have witnessed the argument. Both are disapproving of Jeff's behavior, and the friend who earlier advocated condom use has the final word: "If you really care about a girl, you don't get her pregnant in the first place." Thus, in these 14 minutes, females (Chris, Judy, and the nurse) are represented as emotional, empathetic, and nurturant, while males are mostly irresponsible and insensitive. Chris and Judy are portrayed as abandoned victims, while males are portrayed as having more power in the relationship—the power to leave. Even the more sensitive male friend is positioned in a protective and thus more powerful role than females; as a "responsible" male, he feels he should "take care of" a young woman by using a condom.

Furthermore, the two young women seem to represent a "madonna/whore" duality. Chris looks more feminine, young, vulnerable, and innocent in comparison with Judy, a never-married teenager who smokes cigarettes, looks older than her years, and has just given birth to her second child. Judy seems to have engaged in casual sex without having learned to avoid pregnancy ("Zap! I got pregnant again."). Her boyfriend then abandoned her, and she is bitter about men ("All the guys I've known are creeps."). However, both young women choose to assume the role of mother. In fact, abortion is mentioned only as an unacceptable option that neither could even consider. Adoption is portrayed as an initially plausible but ultimately unsatisfactory decision for Chris, in light of actually giving birth to and seeing her baby; maternal love for her child emerges "naturally."

Thus, the film's depiction of keeping the baby as the option chosen by both young women, along with the absence of discussion of other pregnancy options, invites viewers to see the "natural" and preferable female response to pregnancy as mothering. Although *If You Want To Dance* privileges this option over abortion and adoption, the film simultaneously invites viewers to identify with negative consequences associated with it—desertion by a male partner, economic and emotional difficulties in raising a child alone, and so forth. In so doing, the film also invites the contradictory conclusion that consequences might be *less* negative if adoption or abortion had been chosen.

Finally, the film represents sexual activity exclusively as heterosexual intercourse, silencing other forms of sexual expression, such as masturbation, other heterosexual contact, and gay and lesbian sexual activity. Within this context, the film only briefly mentions condoms as a form of pregnancy prevention and provides no specific information on this or any other method of birth control. Thus, pregnancy might be seen as an inevitable (and negative) outcome of such activity, with abstinence an implicitly legitimated form of avoiding these dire consequences.

In summary, *If You Want To Dance* privileges dominant forms of sexual expression, and stereotypic gender differences, while offering a preferred resolution of teenage pregnancy, that is, keeping the baby. Because its teenage characters are heterosexual, white, and mostly middle class, it excludes the lived experiences of gays and lesbians, students of color, and working-class students. Thus, the film offers these students invisibility rather than a social identity in a wider, diverse community; it may be perceived as de-legitimating their lives. Although its stated goal is promoting male responsibility, the film does not raise the complex and contradictory issues inherent in this broad concept.

As Orner argues in Chapter 3 of this volume, "trigger" films must be discussed in the context of the producers' assumptions about and prescriptions for their use. Student discussion questions in the guide are offered "to help viewers understand and express their feelings, interpret film messages, and discuss important aspects of *If You Want To Dance*" (New Dimension Films, 1983b, p. 1). Eight of the 26 suggested questions are specifically related to personal feelings about situations in the film ["Describe your feelings about the boys' locker room talk" (p. 1); "How do you feel about Chris' decision regarding adoption for her baby?" (p. 2)]. Twelve questions ask for interpretation ["What did Judy mean when she told Chris 'It's the girl that always ends up in the hospital'?" (p. 2); "What did Jeff really mean when he said, 'I've got my whole life ahead of me, and I'm not going to let it go down the tubes just because you got pregnant'?" (p. 2)]. Six questions ask students to apply the film to their own life ["What do you think your life would be like if you were a 15- or 16-year-old father? Mother?" (p. 2); "After viewing this film, how do you feel differently about personal discipline and sexual responsibility? About teenage pregnancy?" (p. 2)]. The latter question, last in the discussion guide, suggests that the film's producers assumed students had a less "disciplined" and "responsible" perception, one that might be changed by watching the film. Taken together with its stated acceptability to parents and members of religious and civic groups, these questions seem designed to "trigger" students to discuss the problematic rather than pleasurable consequences of heterosexual intercourse.

This brief description and interpretation of *If You Want To Dance* is useful for making visible some of its underlying assumptions and ideology of form, content, and intended use as a "trigger." However, since it presumes a context, the film cannot be analyzed in these terms alone. The subsequent discussion of classroom context offers insight into the film's use in a particular classroom as part of a wider sexuality curriculum, selected and presented by a teacher under specific organizational constraints; it also reveals some interpretations and reactions from students who are members of diverse social groups.

CLASSROOM CONTEXT

Before offering my observations of actual classroom presentation and student response to *If You Want To Dance*, it is necessary to briefly describe the setting, classroom teacher, constraints imposed by the organization of the health course, students, and overall teaching strategies resulting from the convergence of these factors.

Van Buren is one of four large public high schools in Woodland, a liberal midwestern city that values education highly and has a local and statewide reputation as a quality educational system. The school, which has been recognized for excellence by the U.S. Department of Education, is located on the less affluent side of Woodland in a residential area of relatively modest homes (most in the $45,000 to $65,000 range) near the city's edge. Most households are supported by state/city government, small business, or blue-collar workers—including many women who work outside the home. The community is homogeneous in terms of race (mostly white) and religion (mostly Christian, including some fundamentalist groups). Traditional values and hierarchical gender arrangements are an integral part of the immediate community and lived culture at Van Buren.

Teacher

The classroom teacher, Mrs. Warren, is a white woman in her mid-thirties who functions in the multiple roles of teacher, mother, and wife. She majored in physical education and minored in health education at a state university, earning two credits short of a major in health and doing well academically. She married while in college and has two children, ages eight and four. With the exception of two maternity leaves, she has been teaching physical education and health at Van Buren for the past twelve years. She helped develop the original district-wide, ninth-grade health curriculum in 1975–76 and taught the course the following year. She is a dedicated, hard-working teacher who is highly regarded among school and district administrative staff as well as her peers; in fact, her reputation as a good sexuality education teacher was an important element in her selection for the study.

Health Course Organization

One-half credit of health education is required for high school graduation in the state where Van Buren is located, so students must pass the ninth-grade health course to graduate. Classes meet daily for a full semester on an alternate classroom/activity basis, that is, even-numbered days in the classroom and odd-numbered days in physical activity. Classroom components of the official district curriculum include healthy lifestyles, physical fitness, nutrition, mental health, human sexuality, personal safety and emergency care, and alcohol and other drugs; physical activity components include jogging, biking, swimming, and weight training. Mrs. Warren has been instrumental in district health curriculum development, and all three Van Buren health teachers attach considerable importance to the district syllabus, attempting to "touch on" all topic areas on approximately the same daily schedule. They are praised by peers and district administration for this consistency.

These and other organizational constraints are a focus of the wider investigation, but will be pursued in considerably less detail here. Based on my observations and interviews over an entire semester, I concluded that these pragmatic/organizational considerations played a major role in Mrs. Warren's teaching strategies. Among these considerations are students' need to pass this required course, a lengthy and continually expanding district syllabus, the fragmented nature of overall teaching duties (Mrs. Warren's schedule included three health classes, four grade levels of physical education, an "adapted" class for special education students), a large number of students (225 a week, 40 in some classes), and a school administrative focus on classroom control and good community relations. Furthermore, the dilemma of finding time and energy to keep up with new information and classroom resources in the rapidly changing, multifaceted field of health—as well as family responsibilities—was continually expressed by Mrs. Warren.

In subsequent sections, I will show how these factors, along with student responses and her personal beliefs, were involved in Mrs. Warren's teaching strategies, including selection and presentation of the film. However, a critique of her teaching strategies is neither intended nor the major issue. Instead, her teaching strategies should be seen and will be explored in more detail as active attempts to cope with organizational dilemmas and minimize student resistance.

Students

There were 27 students (17 females and 10 males) enrolled in Mrs. Warren's second-period health class. About three-fourths of them took academic work fairly seriously (seven had grade averages of 3.5 or higher) and entered to some degree into extracurricular activities; half the males and a third of the females participated in organized school sports, with several students involved in other school-sanctioned activities. In short, most of Mrs. Warren's students met expectations of Van Buren administration and teachers and could be described as "participators." Within this broad category, the most-highly regarded students at Van Buren were "jocks" (those who excelled in sports) and "preppies" (those who were attractive and well-dressed, and usually relatively affluent). The former label was usually associated with males and the latter with females, although not exclusively. Although there were a few "jocks" and "preppies" in the second-period health class, most students were more ordinary "participators." Mrs. Warren referred to them as "good kids."

Nevertheless, a smaller contingent of students did not fit school expectations and norms so well. For example, Mike was the classroom "loner"; this tall, thin, nonathletic young man occasionally interacted with a quiet young woman who sat beside him at the front of the room, but he was more frequently isolated and ridiculed by others—particularly male "jocks"—as (in their words) a "fag."

Three black students (Andrew, Carrie, and Dawn) were another visible group that did not fit prevailing norms at Van Buren (where only 7% are students of color), although they shared characteristics of "participators." Andrew and Carrie frequently engaged in humor and mutual insults with each other that symbolized their bond of intimacy and understanding around race, for example, "you nappy-headed reject from Africa," "African boody-scratcher," and so forth. Carrie and Dawn usually exhibited similar racial solidarity, for example, referring to themselves as "two Negroes" or doing "high fives." However, although Carrie and Dawn shared two aspects of identity (gender and race), there were undercurrents of tension and sometimes caustic classroom exchanges between them. For example, the following incident, which was clearly *not* playful, occurred earlier in the semester while students were matching reactions and substances on a drug worksheet:

DAWN: What's [the reaction to] glue?
CARRIE: Are you dumb! What do you do when you breathe? Does your mama still whup you? If you was mine, I'd whup you everyday 'cause you're so stupid.

DAWN *looks angry, but continues to work silently for a few minutes*
and then says to Carrie: Your lips look crusty because you don't
have lipstick.
CARRIE: Between your legs is crusty.
DAWN: Ooooh, oooh. (*She returns to work.*)

Differences of physical appearance and family income may have ac-
counted for some of the tension between them. First, Carrie's father is
white, and her skin is golden brown—dark enough for her to be considered black by the overwhelmingly white student body and staff, but not
as dark as most other black students, including Dawn. Carrie was—in
her words—"mixed." Thus, her skin color put her outside *both* the dominant white culture and minority culture at Van Buren. Furthermore,
Dawn's slim body, stylish hair, and more expensive clothing (spike heels,
wide leather belts) fit dominant definitions of attractiveness more than
Carrie's chunky body, unruly hair, and less expensive loose tops and
jeans.

A second group that did not fit prevailing school expectations and
norms was the "dirts" (as they were referred to by students and physical
education staff). These students took academic work less seriously, had
their own version of extracurricular activities (including smoking and
"partying"), and were less inclined to follow the rules. Mrs. Warren privately characterized two female students (Paula and Toni) as "dirts,"
largely because they smoked and drank. Both came from working-class
families; Paula had been picked up by the police during that semester for
juvenile drinking, and Toni (as well as her older siblings) had a record of
encounters with school and law enforcement authorities. Toni was a sophomore who was repeating the health class after failing it the previous year.

Along with Carrie and Dawn, Paula and Toni were part of an all-
female social grouping that played the most prominent role in classroom
dynamics. These four usually sat near each other, engaging in muted conversation. When Mrs. Warren separated them, they would simply talk
over another student who was between them or switch seats the following
session.

This group asserted a particular form of "femaleness" in the classroom, cultivating a sophisticated and sexy image. Paula had long bleached
blonde hair, wore heavy make-up, and polished her long manicured nails
in class. Both she and Dawn dressed in ways that accentuated their sexuality, frequently wearing high heeled boots or pumps and tight pants
and sweaters. Furthermore, during nearly every class session, Dawn engaged in a slow, hip-gyrating stroll to the front of the room (to sharpen a
pencil, use the wastebasket), sometimes accompanied by a long leisurely

arm stretch. Toni dressed mostly in tight jeans, a T-shirt (including one with the words, "I got this body from lifting weights—12 ozs. at a time.") or hooded sweatshirt, and sneakers—although she got up very early to "do" her bleached blonde hair.

These three and Carrie (who wore looser clothing) also interjected their sexiness into the classroom in audible ways. The following are representative of numerous similar examples: When Mrs. Warren asked students to list their "favorite activities," Paula asked with feigned innocence, "Can we list things we *really* like to do and not get in trouble?" to which Carrie whispered loudly to Toni, "She'd write 'give blow.'" A few sessions later, when Mrs. Warren solicited qualities looked for in a date, Toni quipped, "We *could* get into details, but I don't think you'd like it." On another occasion, Carrie and Dawn burst into a spontaneous chorus of "I Can't Get No Satisfaction" (with "satis-*fuck*-tion" laughingly substituted by one). Throughout the semester, Carrie kept up a steady stream of humorous digressions and risqué one-liners that perpetuated a sexy image. For example:

"Do we get to practice?" [at the beginning of the sexuality education unit]

A loud "Oh yeah!" [at Mrs. Warren's mention of the female clitoris]

"I'm a sex fiend" [in response to Toni's comment that she had seen Carrie at a shopping mall with several guys]

"Doug [one of the most popular "jocks"], there's a nasty rumor goin' 'round that you and I are layin' down."

Carrie, Dawn, Paula, and Toni also resisted activity sessions in a variety of ways—walking instead of running, forgetting their gym clothes or swim suits, skipping class, fooling around, or recording inflated scores for each other during the physical fitness tests. They did not attempt to hide their dislike for activity, and they participated mainly because they were required to pass—especially Toni, a sophomore who had failed the year before with another teacher, mostly for refusing to get in the swimming pool. In addition, none of them was very good at most activities. As Carrie said to the other three after a paced run, "If I frickin' ran around the world, I couldn't get my pulse over twenty." In short, their lack of interest and skill, minimal enthusiasm, and occasional sullenness during activity was a concern for Mrs. Warren—who saw them as a real "challenge," frequently offered words of encouragement, and genuinely tried to help them pass the course.

As this necessarily brief sketch suggests, the "students" were not a unified coherent group, but smaller, sometimes overlapping, groups with a variety of identities related to gender, class, race, sexual preference, appearance, and so on. Thus, the classroom was a social arena in which contradictions and tensions between and within groups worked their way through daily school life. On the whole, few students offered straightforward challenges to information Mrs. Warren presented or to her agenda, although even the "good kids" conducted their own informal, sometimes raunchy, exchanges during Mrs. Warren's presentations. Students generally regarded the class as easy and exerted enough effort in activity and the classroom to get A's and B's, while keeping levels of informality and jocularity within limits acceptable to Mrs. Warren. As the following comments illustrate, most students recognized the implicit classroom bargain:

> LAUREN: If you just lay back, you would get a "C." If you try hard and really do what she asks, you'll get an "A."
>
> ANDREW: Even the lowest person—if they don't do really bad—will pass. A lotta teachers don't want to flunk kids, but some teachers are more prone to *do* something about it. If you know something in health, you'll pass—and Mrs. Warren helps you get a better score.

Furthermore, four female students in two of the marginal groups (students of color and "dirts") played a major role in renegotiating this bargain and influencing classroom process. They contested reified school knowledge about sexuality and classroom control by engaging in a variety of visible, interactive, and collective activities. These attempts to make the classroom more relevant and livable took various forms, including accentuating female sexuality, making humorous quips, initiating conversational eruptions, and interjecting their own cultural experience and language into the classroom. However, as anecdotal evidence from the film presentation will exemplify, their contestation and Mrs. Warren's responses were generally good-natured and humorous rather than belligerent. More theoretically, Everhart (1983) uses the term "regenerative knowledge" to describe the way of knowing that emerges as students reinterpret school knowledge in the context of their own cultural experiences. As I shall elaborate next, keeping these forms of regenerative knowledge under control was another factor in Mrs. Warren's teaching strategies.

Teaching Strategies

Given the organizational constraints and student cultural responses just outlined, Mrs. Warren needed to achieve a balance between covering material on a lengthy district syllabus and making the work easy enough for students to do well; between creating an atmosphere of fun and encouraging students to take the class seriously; between maintaining classroom control and being enough of a "buddy" to secure student participation in physical activities. In the context of these pressures, she gained student compliance and maintained a congenial authority by utilizing what McNeil (1986) calls "defensive teaching" strategies. In short, she controlled students by controlling knowledge: selecting noncontroversial topics, simplifying content, presenting mostly fragments of technical detail, and limiting discussion. For example, during the five and one-half hours of classroom time on sexuality (the last and shortest unit of the semester), Mrs. Warren focused on such noncontroversial topics as dating, communicating with parents, adolescent body changes, reproductive anatomy and physiology, negative consequences of heterosexual intercourse (sexually transmitted diseases and teenage pregnancy), and saying "no" to intercourse. These took up over three-quarters of class time, while sexual response/pleasure, masturbation, abortion, and homosexuality were barely mentioned.

Although she addressed the somewhat more controversial topic of birth control (30 minutes, including 7 minutes showing the various items), Mrs. Warren presented this and other information mostly as technical details, easily transmitted and graded on exams. For example, she listed an "effectiveness" percentage for each method without defining the term, but she did not explain how methods were used. She frequently read aloud from informational handouts and provided brief answers for student worksheets, explicitly pointing out items on which students would be tested during "review" sessions. Even topics characterized by several "correct" responses were reduced to one acceptable answer for the exam, for example, "Good communication between husband and wife is the basis for building a good family relationship." Like Mrs. Warren's explanations, class discussions consisted mainly of fragments, with some students calling out brief remarks related to her questions; there were no structured small-group discussions. I never observed substantive or ongoing large-group discussion guided by student questions, although the students did ask some questions that Mrs. Warren answered, frequently about her personal and family life. Given her status as heterosexual, wife, and mother, these personal asides implicitly conferred status on dominant cultural values, particularly since students liked her and the class. Nevertheless, some of her comments (she made more money than her husband and their children are in day care) did contradict traditional gender arrangements. Thus, rich and diverse knowledge about sexuality was reduced to a narrow range of largely noncontroversial, technical school knowledge with little relevance to students. As expressed by one young woman, course content was "just stuff you had to know. I don't know if we'll ever use it."

More theoretically, cultural knowledge was reduced to "reified" knowledge, a term Robert Everhart (1983) uses for knowledge forms that pervade schooling and underpin empirical science. He maintains that knowledge is based on linear/causal relationships, with abstract and problematic knowledge treated as if it is concrete and factual. "Facts" are what is to be "learned," while their problematic nature, assumptions behind them, or criteria for selection are not explored. Thus, like the educational system in general, details about sexuality became a reified version of an abstract, value-laden, and controversial issue. There was little room for meaningful student dialogue with presented information, and its manipulation (writing it down and recalling it for exams) was more significant for students than its exploration.

It is worth noting that students overwhelmingly expressed satisfaction with the content and methods in the sex education unit and with the class as a whole. For example, when asked what they would tell friends about the class, 15 students (including Carrie, Dawn, and Paula) offered such superlatives as "The teacher's real cool," "Mrs. Warren is the nicest teacher," "I hope you [the friend] get Mrs. Warren," and "It was fun— one of my best classes." It bears repeating that my intent is not to criticize Mrs. Warren's teaching strategies as they relate to the film but to describe its use, beginning with preview and selection, in the context of specific institutional dilemmas and student responses.

THE FILM IN USE

Preview and Selection

If You Want To Dance was previewed by ten health teachers from all four Woodland high schools at a half-day district inservice near the beginning of the semester. Such meetings were rare on school days, since the district had to pay for substitutes at every school. However, in light of the district-wide evaluation process in health and the publicity during the summer of 1985 on school AIDS curriculums, the district administrator for health and physical education arranged for this meeting. The lengthy agenda included revision of course objectives for all seven classroom topic areas (an item that was not finished that day and teachers agreed to complete as "homework") and other district business.

In addition, a consultant from a local cooperative education service agency was invited to make teachers aware of available resource materials on AIDS. After a brief presentation, handouts, and a videotape on this topic, the consultant told teachers she wanted their opinion on another film and introduced *If You Want To Dance* by saying, "It's a film recommended for high schools—that's all I'm going to say about it." She handed out an evaluation form requiring response and comments in three areas ("Quality of Material," "Appropriate Usage of Material," and "Possible Concepts to Be Learned from Material") and turned on the projector, and the teachers silently watched *If You Want To Dance.*

The following summary, with excerpts from field notes, describes events after the film: Before the credits finish, Mrs. Warren enthusiastically announces that she "really likes" the film and asks where to get it. The consultant replies that it was made by the U.S. Department of Health and Human Services and is owned by her agency. She says that 65 teachers at a workshop the previous summer made a "unanimous decision" that it should be purchased, and a later advisory board had "some interesting reactions." Then she asks, "Were there any stereotypes of males?" Three of the five men are talking among themselves and do not hear the question; a female teacher says that the film "attempted to put both sides in." The consultant replies, "My chin fell to the floor the first time I saw it."

There is no group focus as teachers (particularly those from the same schools) talk among themselves about the film. The consultant refocuses the group, announcing that the film and a resource catalog are available free of charge from her agency and providing the phone number. A male teacher, who is teaching health for the first time, raises a question about how the film compares with another on teenage pregnancy currently owned by the district. The other teachers respond that the older film "deals more with the family context" and "a guy's decision-making process."

> MALE TEACHER: Is it okay to show both without overdoing it?
> CONSULTANT: It's not too much. Sometimes we underestimate our young people. You might get them to evaluate.

A female teacher says she would like to use *If You Want To Dance;* her male colleague at the same school turns to her and asks, "Don't you think it's anti-abortion? Once you see babies pictured like cute little puppies?" The female teacher replies, "I'm not sure. Maybe that's the underlying message." She goes on to say that she sees this message as "secondary." "The main thing is, it focuses on the sex act." The male teacher looks peevish, but does not respond verbally.

Meanwhile, the three Van Buren teachers discuss *when*—not

whether—to use the film. Mrs. Warren consults her schedule, and they request it for the first week in December. Teachers from two other schools join in, saying they want it too and could do their sexuality unit then. The consultant replies, "How about I send it here from December 2–13, and you can ship it around to all the Woodland Schools?" Teachers respond with a chorus of "Great," "Thanks," and so forth. They quickly choose particular days and record the dates in their notebooks.

The consultant collects evaluation forms, which most teachers have been filling out by checking the appropriate responses, making only brief comments. Mrs. Warren rates the film "Excellent." The consultant thanks the teachers for their help, gathers her materials, and leaves; the group moves on to the next agenda item.

Total "discussion" time for the film was about eight minutes. As this description demonstrates, there was no conceptual introduction and no substantive group discussion of teacher interpretation, possible student responses, or suggestions for classroom use. Teachers mostly conducted their own informal small-group conversations rather than participating in group deliberation, with time constraints imposed by the crowded meeting agenda serving as a barrier to lengthy substantive discussion. As I shall demonstrate next, these same dynamics characterized presentation of the film in Mrs. Warren's classroom.

I asked Mrs. Warren the following day what criteria she used to evaluate the film, and she replied that "language at the kids' level" was most important; language should be "not too technical." She added that it "works best" when material is presented by young people rather than an expert adult like the doctor in the AIDS videotape at the previous day's inservice. She went on to say that *If You Want To Dance* was "more real. It showed how it *really* is. Guys really talk that way." Although I learned later in the semester that Mrs. Warren was opposed to abortion, she did not at this point mention her opposition as a factor in film selection and never directly told students that abortion was an unacceptable pregnancy option.

Nevertheless, this personal stance did enter into some of Mrs. Warren's other curricular choices during the sexuality unit. For example, at a later session on pregnancy and prenatal development, she showed the class several magazine color photographs that illustrated various stages of fetal development. In response to several students' initial exclamations of "gross," "yuck," and so forth, she replied, "They're beautiful. There's a miracle going on here." She immediately added that last year a student had asked if these were pictures of abortions, and went on to tell students that the pictures were of either miscarriages or live "babies" within the woman's body, taken by special photographic techniques. She then passed around the photographs, pointing out such details as the umbilical cord ("the lifeline between the baby and the mother") and a fetus with thumb near its mouth, mostly referring to the fetus as "baby." In a subsequent interview, Mrs. Warren revealed that she consciously used the prenatal pictures as an implicit statement against abortion.

While *If You Want To Dance* did reinforce Mrs. Warren's antiabortion sentiments, it contradicted her belief that adoption is the preferable choice for a pregnant teen. In fact, she stopped inviting teenage mothers from the district's school-age maternity program to speak to her classes because of their "pushing" to keep the baby, an option also clearly "pushed" by the film. Since *If You Want To Dance* both reinforced and contradicted Mrs. Warren's personal values about pregnancy options, it is not accurate to assert that she selected the film as an ideological vehicle. Instead, as the data suggest, she and other Woodland health teachers collectively decided to use this film more for reasons related to availability, scheduling, and perceived relevance to students than to its ideological message. Similarly, the wider study suggests that Mrs. Warren's personal beliefs about sexuality did consciously enter into some of her curricular decisions, including her exclusion of homosexuality from the curriculum except for mentioning it as the highest "risk group" for AIDS. Her own ambiguity about a gay relative ("I'm not afraid of him, but I'm not comfortable with him") surfaced during the interviews. However, as was the case with abortion, other factors related to organizational constraints and potential student response also played a role in this exclusion. Taken together, my observations and interviews suggest that personal beliefs had less effect on the sexuality curriculum in use than these other factors.

Classroom Presentation

If You Want To Dance was shown to students in all of Van Buren's health classes on the agreed-upon date in early December, the third session in a nine-session sexuality unit. Adhering to the schedule meant that the film on teenage pregnancy came immediately after physical changes of adolescence and before dating and the menstrual cycle, as the following list of session dates and topics illustrates:

December 4	Child/parent relationships
December 6	Marriage and family; physical changes of adolescence
December 10	Teenage pregnancy (film)

December 12	Quiz on family/physical changes of adolescence; menstrual cycle; dating
December 16	Qualities looked for in a date; love vs. infatuation; saying "no" to intercourse
December 18	Advantages/disadvantages of "going with" one person; teenage marriage; female/male reproductive anatomy
December 20	Pregnancy/prenatal development; childbirth; birth control devices
January 6	Birth control; sexually transmitted diseases
January 8	Sexually transmitted diseases; fourth degree sexual assault; exam review

This seemingly random order, absence of transition between topics, and a two-week Christmas vacation all contributed to an overall impression of fragmentation. Furthermore, this sequence of topics was interrupted on a daily basis by Mrs. Warren's giving directions, answering questions, or presenting material regarding alternate-day physical activities such as fitness tests, timed runs, and weight training.

Introducing the film. Such was the case on the day the film was shown. Students were scheduled to begin work in the weight room the day after it was scheduled, so Mrs. Warren used the first 25 minutes of class to explain various muscle groups, using an overhead projector and worksheets. When I later asked about the rationale for this, Mrs. Warren replied, "It just happened; that wasn't planned right . . . the muscle groups were something I had to get done." The following excerpts from my field notes detail classroom events after this presentation was completed:

MRS. WARREN: We're seeing a movie today. It's called, *If You Want To Dance.* It's a film on teenage pregnancy. (*She goes on to describe the beginning and its shift between a basketball court and delivery room, with father in one place and mother in another.*) The delivery is nothing drastic, but you will see the baby coming out. (*Two male students stand and request permission to go to the bathroom. Mrs. Warren tells them to sit down.*)
FEMALE STUDENT: Doesn't he [the father] want it?
MRS. WARREN: No. There are a number of people pregnant in this school. There's a sophomore who's still here in school, a senior who will deliver in about a month, a freshman . . .
SEVERAL STUDENTS: Who?

MRS. WARREN: No names. We'll tie this [the film] into what we've
been talking about. More on relationships Thursday [the next
classroom session] and then to reproduction stuff. I'm assuming
you know a lot, but I'm not so sure.

A few girls at the front say they have seen a filmed delivery,
and Mrs. Warren speaks personally to them. Meanwhile, Mr. Austin
[another health teacher] is opening the divider that separates the
large classroom he shares with Mrs. Warren, and she moves to help
[they have agreed in advance that this will happen at a certain
time]. As the divider is opened, students from the two classes call
out greetings to each other and noisily move their chairs to Mrs.
Warren's half of the room. Mr. Austin wheels the projector into
place, a student turns out the lights, and the film begins with no
further teacher comment. Students immediately become quiet.

Watching the film. Most students were quiet, attentive, and focused
on the screen during the film. Their facial expressions showed minimal
affect; on the whole, they looked attentively neutral, a generalization that
was true for screenings I observed in two other classes (however, as data
from subsequent student interviews will reveal, there was considerable
complexity behind this apparently neutral attentiveness). There were
also moments of inattention and contestation: Mike doodled on some papers; Dawn read from a paperback during the first five minutes; Andrew
and Carrie whispered briefly to each other. Paula occasionally called out
responses to lines from the actors. For example, when Chris asks Judy if
she is/ever was married, Paula responded with a loud "No" to both questions. When Judy says, "Zap! I got pregnant again," Paula spoke an em-
phatic "Yes." When Chris tells Judy that she [Chris] probably looks old
too, Paula called out, "About 10." A few of Paula's friends from Mr. Austin's class who were sitting nearby laughed softly at these remarks, but
no one else responded. There were two points in the film when several
students laughed; the first occurred when Jeff ogles the nurse as he asks
direction to Chris' room. Second, when Chris calls the nurse to ask to see
her baby, a student imitated her in a high-pitched, whiny voice, prompt-
ing laughter from others.

Mrs. Warren stood and leaned against a radiator at the side of the
room during the movie. From my vantage point next to her, I could feel
her emotional involvement. She focused intently on the screen (sometimes with a pained expression), arms folded tightly across her chest and
body rigid. She gave me several intense looks, and just before Chris and
Judy begin their hospital conversation, she said loudly to the students,
"Now *listen* to this." She was similarly involved in the film during another

of her classes I observed the same day, whispering to me during the delivery scene, "This just brings back so many memories."

As the film ended, one student called out, "What a stupid ending." Mr. Austin turned on the lights, and the noise level increased as his students returned chairs to their half of the classroom. The two teachers moved the divider back in place, with eight minutes left in the class period. Mrs. Warren walked to the front of her half of the room, holding the discussion guide that came with the film.

Discussing the film. In keeping with the general pattern of fragmented student discussion described previously, discussion after the film consisted of Mrs. Warren asking questions and students calling out brief responses. As was also true during other sessions, Carrie, Dawn, Paula, and Toni were the most active participants. The following excerpt from my field notes demonstrates how these four marginalized students contested the film's points of view by interjecting humor, as well as alternate knowledge, beliefs, and lived experiences into classroom discourse. It also illustrates the overall fragmented nature of discussion, students' ultimate redirection of classroom discourse, and Mrs. Warren's attempts to redirect the focus by formulating alternate questions and drawing on her own adult experience in giving birth.

> MRS. WARREN: What did you think of it [the film]?
>
> MALE STUDENT: You should put your money in the jukebox [a play on words spoken by Jeff's responsible friend in the film, "If you want to dance, you have to put your money in the jukebox"]. (*Several students laugh, apparently at the possible double meaning.*)
>
> CARRIE (*suggesting that Chris might have had an abortion*): You can get them until you're six months pregnant.
>
> MRS. WARREN: I know you can, but . . .
>
> DAWN: Who'd wanna have adoption after nine months? (*Several students have begun talking among themselves, and the group focus disappears. This goes on for about a minute.*)
>
> MRS. WARREN (*loudly*): Put yourself in the girl or guy's place.
>
> TONI: I'd slap him [the teenage father] up.
>
> CARRIE (*sarcastically*): I'd be the sweetest girl in the world.
>
> PAULA (*defiantly*): My mom was 17 when she had me.
>
> TONI: My mom was married when she was 18, and she got married because she had my sister.
>
> CARRIE: My sister had a baby when she was 14.
>
> DAWN: My cousin had a baby when she was 14.

> *They more or less call their comments out into the air, while several other students begin to talk with each other. Mrs. Warren speaks with a small group of young women in the front, and the group focus vanishes again. This goes on for about a minute.*
>
> *Mrs. Warren looks at the discussion guide and asks, in a loud voice, what message the film was trying to give by switching back and forth at the beginning from the basketball scene to the delivery room [I later notice that this is the first question in the guide] . . . although they didn't really show much of the birth.*
> MALE STUDENT: Yeah, the censored version.
> MRS. WARREN: The guy in the film said girls know about their own bodies, but they [guys] have no idea what the pain's like during birth—no idea. I felt like my back was coming through my skin. I had back labor. *(She elaborates on her own delivery for several seconds and points out that Jeff seemed "uncomfortable" in the hospital. She says the film is going to Butler [another Woodland high school] and that Bonnie [the researcher] will be taking it.)*
> *This launches a series of questions from students, directed at me, for example, "Where do you teach?" "How can you come every morning?" "Do you get paid?" When I say "No" to this, several students exclaim, "Really?" Mrs. Warren says it seems fair for students to ask me questions, since I get to ask them. This interaction—with me as focus—occupies the last minute before the bell rings. As students leave, Mrs. Warren tells them she thinks she will show the film a second time.*

However, *If You Want To Dance* is never mentioned or referred to again in the classroom.

Later that day, Mrs. Warren commented to me on her perception of student reactions: "Second hour [the class described here] perceived it as a story—not as something that could happen to them. Fourth hour [a later class] was much better." Furthermore, she told me and another health teacher at lunch that "second hour was in favor of abortion," generalizing to the whole class from Dawn's and Carrie's comments. I had also observed fourth hour, and these students were more quiet during the film; no one contested the film's point of view and several (at least 7) students asked Mrs. Warren questions about her personal opinion and life. For example,

> MRS. WARREN: What would you do if you were the girl?
> FEMALE STUDENT: Keep it.

FEMALE STUDENT: How old were you when you had your first kid?

MRS. WARREN: 27. And I was still not really sure I wanted kids. I was teaching then, and my students were kind of like my kids. But I was afraid of getting too old.

FEMALE STUDENT: You're never too old.

MRS. WARREN: Over 35, there are lots of complications.

FEMALE STUDENT: If you were 17, what would you do?

MRS. WARREN: If I were 17, I would've put it up for adoption. That would probably be easier, although for the girl, she'd always have that feeling that part of her was somewhere else. . . . It's pretty hard to go through school having little ones around. (*She goes on to describe the cost of day care [$5,000 for her two children] and her own hectic morning schedule.*)

The preceding description of the use of *If You Want To Dance* in a particular sexuality education classroom shows the selection and presentation of educational media to be a complex and sometimes contradictory process that is embedded in a wider curriculum in use. It reveals some of the practical considerations related to district, school, and subject-matter constraints that influenced Mrs. Warren's use of defensive teaching strategies. As the wider study documents more fully, simplified and fragmented content, noncontroversial topics, and limited student discussion are partial solutions to the structural dilemmas she encountered. They represent active attempts to negotiate organizational constraints.

This description of classroom process around educational media illuminates the classroom as a social arena, highlighting the contradictions and tensions between and within various social groupings that permeate it. It suggests student capacity to influence the construction of daily classroom experience. In the next section, I shall use interview data to elaborate on student classroom response, examining students' active negotiation of the film's meaning and attempts to act in their own best interests. Finally, I will discuss the sometimes contradictory effects of their actions.

STUDENT INTERPRETATIONS

Interviews after the sexuality education unit made clear that they did not passively internalize its major points of view but constructed multiple, sometimes contradictory versions. Furthermore, interviews showed student classroom behavior during and after the film to have numerous meanings, not readily apparent from observations. Finally, interviews revealed that students actively weighed their own interests in acquiescing to or contesting the film's content and classroom procedures. For some (mostly "participators"), this meant outwardly acquiescing to information and procedures in order to get a good grade in the required course and to avoid embarrassment, while reinterpreting the film's messages. For more marginalized students (especially Carrie, Dawn, Paula, and Toni), it meant visibly and collectively contesting the film's points of view; nevertheless, they did this in ways that did not push Mrs. Warren too far and avoided the risk of personal embarrassment.

Film's Major Message

Students were asked specifically during the interview, "What do you see as the major message of the film?" While their responses did not fit neatly into categories, the largest number of interpretations clustered around warning teenagers of the negative consequences of teenage pregnancy. The following comments were typical of the 12 students (8 females, 4 males) offering this broad interpretation:

Females

"Havin' a baby is trouble. It causes problems."
"You should think of the consequences."
"That you should think before taking that big of a step—having intercourse and choosing what to do about a pregnancy."
"To warn teenagers of what their responsibilities are."

Males

"It kinda put a scare in you about teenage pregnancy."
"If you're ready to go for it, you should be prepared for all the consequences that might happen."

Six students (5 females, 1 male) perceived the main point of the film in generally the same way as the discussion guide—promoting male responsibility. Carrie most colorfully summarized her interpretation of the film's male-directed message: "Don't be a dick." However, only one young man referred specifically to the male role in pregnancy *prevention* as the film's primary focus: "Guys should use birth control." In contrast, two young women referred to a male's responsibility in dealing with rather than preventing pregnancy: "If a guy gets a girl pregnant, he shouldn't just leave her alone. It's kind of his responsibility too."

In addition, three young men saw the main point as intended for *both* sexes: "say 'no' to intercourse," "mutual responsibility," and "take precautions." Finally, two young women turned the intended message of male responsibility on its head. Instead, they reinterpreted its major point as a woman's right to decide what to do about a pregnancy, rejecting the less powerful role of women offered by the film.

> "It's the woman's body. She should do what she thinks is right. If he says, 'Get rid of it,' she should still keep it if she wants to."
> "It's up to the girl to decide because they went to all the trouble having it."

Nevertheless, it is worth noting that both implicitly subscribed to another of the film's and teacher's points of view, the notion that the woman would want to keep the baby.

Mike (the classroom "loner") characterized the major message of *If You Want To Dance* as "bogus" and was the only student who said he would not recommend showing the film other semesters. This student's interview responses and classroom interactions will be described in some detail because they illustrate (as did several others) that "quiet" attention during the film did not signify acceptance of its points of view. Furthermore, in spite of his almost complete classroom silence during the sexuality unit, Mike was one of several "quiet" students who offered lengthy, thoughtful responses to interview questions. As I shall later demonstrate, this potential for student analysis was not utilized in the classroom partly because students believed it was not a safe place to speak on this issue. The following excerpt describes Mike's response to the question, "What do you see as the major purpose of the film?"

> It was bogus. (*pause*) If you're going to be sexually active, A: Be prepared and use birth control. B: If you are pregnant, you have to make a choice. . . . [I] kept expecting to see part two [since the movie] gave no insight into the decisions already made. (*Mike goes on to describe a network television situation comedy that he thought provided better coverage of teenage pregnancy. He explains that characters in the television program were closer to ninth grade, in contrast to the somewhat older teens in the classroom film. Furthermore, he believes that the network show has a second advantage*): [It gave more insight into] the *process* of making the decision of what to do about a pregnancy. (*Mike says he remembers the last line of the television show*): "Whatever she decides [to do about the pregnancy], her life will never be the same." (*He tells me he has the show on videotape and offers to let me watch it.*)

Mike did bring in the videotape; after I watched it, we met after school to discuss it and to complete the interview. I was impressed, as I had been during our first interaction, with his level of knowledge and thoughtful articulation of sexuality issues. Mike was one of the students most critical of the sexuality unit, believing that myths should be explicitly debunked in the classroom because they are so widespread among adolescents. He also expressed a preference for more classroom coverage of such controversial topics as sexual response, birth control, sexual assault, pregnancy choices, and homosexuality. With regard to the latter, Mike said: "Kids have to deal with this—maybe not directly, but they have to deal with it. If you don't cover it, you have myths again. . . . There's not a great big percent of this around here, but it's rising."

In response to the question, "What would have to happen in the classroom for you to be comfortable discussing the issues raised by the film?" Mike said that his own comfort about sexuality was not a factor in his decision not to participate in classroom discussion. Instead, he perceived Mrs. Warren as ill at ease with certain topics: "Mrs. Warren didn't seem comfortable talking about some things, like male birth control—plus all the things she didn't cover."

In short, interviews with students suggested that *If You Want To Dance* did not "transmit" a monolithic message unilaterally "received" by students. Instead, they variously reinterpreted its "major message" in ways that contradicted each other as well as the expressed intent of the film. Furthermore, as typified by Mike, the thoughtfulness and depth of interview responses stood in marked contrast to the level of student classroom participation. As I shall describe in the following section, interviews also revealed a complex array of meanings behind students' mostly attentive and acquiescent classroom responses during and after the film as well as during the rest of the sexuality unit.

Classroom Dynamics

When asked specifically, "What did the quiet during the movie mean for you?" about 70% (12 of 13 females; 4 of 10 males) of interviewed students, including Andrew, Carrie, Dawn, and Paula, said they were, in Paula's words, "into it" for a variety of reasons. These centered around the film's realistic representation of issues students perceive to be relevant. The following comments were typical:

"That situation could really happen."
"There were teenagers—not adults—in it."

"They're doin' exactly what somebody would do."
"People in the movie were the same as ordinary people in school."

Three young women volunteered that males were accurately portrayed as "mean," "being a geek," and a "dick." In the words of one, "Most
guys are like that." Two young women said they were thinking during the
movie about what would happen if they were to become pregnant as
teenagers: "It would be awful if it ever happened." One studious and shy
young man said he was interested even though the film "didn't apply [to
him at this point]. . . . I'm not too worried about getting anyone pregnant."

In short, most students, particularly young women, said they were
quiet during *If You Want To Dance* because they were at least somewhat
involved in the film for reasons of interest or applicability. Several volunteered that they took it seriously. Furthermore, when asked what they
thought the quiet during the film meant for other students, most believed
their classmates were silent for similar reasons. In general, this contradicts Mrs. Warren's sense that second-hour students believed the film
was not applicable to them.

Interviews revealed other complexities behind this outwardly acquiescent student behavior, with six students (1 female, 5 males) saying
they were quiet for reasons distinctly different from interest or applicability. Some described themselves as "bored" during the film or quiet
because of specific classroom constraints. For example,

"I never goof around in this class; there are no people to do it with."
"I usually don't talk during movies. You usually get caught 'cause not
    too many other people talk."

Thus, as was true for other classroom sessions, students seemed to silently but actively calculate their own best interests by keeping their part
in the implicit classroom bargain—acceptable behavior in exchange for
an easy grade in the required course.

Embarrassment—or at least the potential for it—was another factor
in the "quiet" I observed during the film, as well as during other sessions
in the sexuality unit. In fact, 80% of the interviewed young women and
70% of the young men specifically commented, without solicitation from
me, on the potential for embarrassment as a factor in their classroom
sexuality education experience. Most students (85%) said they would
have preferred more audiovisuals in the sexuality unit and offered a variety of reasons, including specific mention of avoiding embarrassment.

In the words of one student who wanted more films in the unit, "You can just watch 'em; you don't have to talk to them [other students] about it."

Thus, during the sexuality unit, most students did not participate in class discussion, but confined themselves to muted exchanges with those nearby. The following comments illustrate their worry about embarrassment:

> "Hardly anyone talks. They may be embarrassed. I know I would."
> "If you're in a large group, you really don't want to talk because you feel people will laugh at you or something."

In fact, near the end of the interview, students were asked, "What would have to happen in the classroom for you to be comfortable talking about the issues raised by the film?" Nearly one-third of those interviewed about the film (23% of females and 40% of males) said that *nothing* could make them comfortable talking about such issues in a classroom. As one young man succinctly summarized, "I can't imagine talking about it in a classroom. I'll listen and think, but not talk."

Humor and embarrassment. As previously described, the "girls" (particularly Carrie) actively participated, often through use of humor, in contesting reified knowledge about sexuality as well as classroom control. As described earlier, Carrie's humorous quips reinforced membership in peer groups related to gender and race. In addition, she used humor to seek a privileged relationship with Mrs. Warren, while simultaneously contesting the teacher's authority. For example, she used familiar terms of address such as "buddy" and "babe," asked Mrs. Warren questions about her family, teased her ("I say we call out the hickey inspector" [to investigate a red mark on Mrs. Warren's neck]), offered compliments ("You're pretty hip for an old lady"), and stopped after class to tell personal anecdotes. Mrs. Warren usually responded in a good-natured way to this informality and humor, once answering Carrie's "Thank you, babe" with a "You're welcome, babe." Furthermore, there were several occasions when Mrs. Warren (and everyone else in the room, including me) simply could not keep from laughing at Carrie's one-liners. Carrie did not usually push Mrs. Warren too far, responding to the teacher's gentle admonitions and reserving her most caustic or obscene comments for muted exchanges with other students, especially Paula. In short, Carrie was a key factor in the bantering classroom atmosphere—shifting the boundaries of discussion from technical details to irreverent humor, entertaining students plus teacher and guest, initiating barrages of humorous one-liners from classmates, and genially contesting Mrs. Warren's authority.

Carrie was by no means alone in her attempts to make the classroom more livable. Most students participated, in the form of muted humorous exchanges with others seated nearby. However, these ebullient outbursts, which generally seemed to subside spontaneously, contributed to an overall air of levity in the classroom. Several students expressed concern about being laughed at by other students, a fear that was partially warranted by the general level of jocularity, humorous one-liners, and occasional put-downs that occurred. The hurtful potential of classroom "humor" was made visible throughout the semester by some students' treatment of Mike, the classroom "loner." On many occasions, he was the butt of name-calling (including "nerd," "queer," and "fag"), insults ("His Mom gives him a hand job"), and threats ("I say we all get in line and back-hand him once"). These comments came most frequently from males, especially from one of the most popular "jocks." Most other students (again, especially males) laughed loudly at these remarks, while Mike (who sat at the front among the quieter young women) always looked straight ahead and remained silent. When I asked the interview question, "What comments can you make on student behavior?" Mike said, "I don't know. I didn't pay too much attention."

Mrs. Warren was usually absorbed elsewhere and never commented on or intervened in these situations. These remarks, the general laughter that followed, and the fact that no one challenged them made fear of embarrassment reasonable in this classroom. Therefore, although Mike was articulately critical of the film and sexuality unit during the interview, he said virtually nothing in class. Although he did not express this explicitly, my observations suggest that Mike was silent because this classroom was not a safe place for his voice to be heard.

Even the male "jock" who most frequently tormented Mike expressed concern about other students' perceptions. He thought the sexuality textbook should be available for students to read at home so that others would not "bug you" for being "curious." "In school, others might think they don't know if they're too interested." Thus, these dynamics also collectively reinforced stereotypic versions of masculinity as well as heterosexuality.

Feigned disinterest. Other students expressed concern about having their interest and participation in the sexuality education unit misinterpreted by students or teacher. As the following examples suggest, young women were concerned about looking too "experienced," with stereotypic sex roles a factor in the kind of embarrassment they might experience. For example, a female student who had just transferred to Van Buren from a smaller school that offered no school sexuality education told me that she deliberately masked her classroom interest in sexuality information, especially birth control. Thus, she sat quietly, looked bored, and was perceived by Mrs. Warren as totally disinterested. However, this young woman revealed to me that she had learned a great deal from the class and offered the following insight on her own behavior, which she felt applied to other students (male and female) as well:

> Everybody's putting on this cool act to give the impression you don't really care. You don't need to care because you're "Jack Cool." But if you look too interested, that's not good either. People will wonder what you're doing.

After learning that I had worked at Planned Parenthood, she privately asked me several questions about birth control and later said, "I'm not gonna stand up in the middle of class and say, 'I wanna know about birth control.' They'd think I was using it." She believed that this would give her a bad "reputation" at this new school.

Although Carrie, Dawn, Paula, and Toni promoted an image of sexual sophistication, they revealed very little *personal* behavior or feelings in class. For example, in the excerpt of the post-film discussion quoted earlier, all four contested the film's points of view by offering life experiences of *other* family members rather than asserting a personal belief that teenage pregnancy and parenthood are not wholly negative events. Dawn also chose not to ask questions about birth control in class and expressed this concern.

> DAWN: Students might react or have a reaction. I'm not comfortable saying it in front of an adult—unless they don't know who I am. They might think I'm doing something. (*pause*) The teacher might wonder why you asked and do something.
> INTERVIEWER: Do you mean refer you to a guidance counselor—or something like that?
> DAWN: Yes. Even my mom gets uptight when I ask questions like that. She thinks I'm obscene.

Her suspicions about school personnel were warranted; I had learned earlier from another staff person at Van Buren that this young woman's name (along with four others) had been forwarded by the middle school she had attended in response to requests for names of students potentially "at risk for pregnancy." (Her previously discussed cultivation of a sexy image as well as racism may have been factors in this assessment.)

*   *   *

As I have described in this section, Mrs. Warren's students were active participants in interpreting the film's meaning and constructing the experience of its classroom presentation. Although most did not overtly challenge the film's information or values, interviews revealed that they arrived at their own varied meanings of its major message. Furthermore, while most outwardly acquiesced to classroom arrangements, they actively calculated their own best interests—especially getting a good grade in the required course, making the classroom more livable, and avoiding embarrassment.

Students from marginalized groups most visibly contested the film's point of view, including the notion of sexuality and teenage pregnancy as adult-owned experiences with totally negative consequences. Furthermore, they were instrumental in creating a humorous, bantering classroom climate that had the potential to make a "joke" out of any sexuality topic, however serious. At the end of class, students were briefly able to expand the parameters of discussion to accommodate their language and cultural experience, becoming co-definers of classroom discourse.

However, the "humorous" insults and potential for embarrassment inherent in this atmosphere seemed to have contradictory effects. While humor and insults defined peer boundaries and made the classroom more livable, the potential for embarrassment also meant that even the most vocal students bracketed personal information and refrained from asking questions (especially those with personal relevance) or expressing points of view that might be ridiculed by others. It was safer for most students to keep quiet. In addition, it was difficult for Mrs. Warren to ascertain what information students may have already known; the cavalier attitude and cultivation of a sexy image by some female students may have given the impression that they "knew" more (in terms of both information and experience) than they actually did. Finally, as more fully documented in the wider study, student creation of a humorous, bantering environment had the unintended and contradictory effect of partially triggering defensive teaching strategies that ultimately made classroom knowledge about sexuality less relevant to the students' needs. Put more broadly, cultural resistance that was liberating at one level actually contributed to the students' subordination at another.

CONCLUSION

This close-up description and analysis of *If You Want To Dance* and its use in Mrs. Warren's classroom illustrates that the points of view around sexuality, gender relations, and pregnancy options encoded in the film were mostly consistent with norms of dominant groups. It privileged white, middle-class heterosexuality; portrayed pregnancy as an inevitable outcome of (hetero)sexual activity; offered keeping the baby as the preferred choice after pregnancy; and invited viewers to accept stereotypic gender roles and an unbridgeable communication gap between the sexes. Nevertheless, the data suggest that teachers did not select the film solely on the basis of agreement with these points of view, and students did not passively accept them. There were moments of questioning and contradiction for both teacher and students.

Instead of selection and transmission of ideology to passive objects, the data illuminate a more dynamic and tentative process, in which both Mrs. Warren and her students actively made decisions on their own behalf. Mrs. Warren attempted to cope with organizational dilemmas and to minimize student resistance by using defensive teaching strategies—selecting noncontroversial topics, presenting easily transmitted and graded fragments of information, and limiting student discussion. These had the unintended consequence of reducing rich cultural knowledge about sexuality to reified school knowledge, mostly irrelevant to students' lives. In this context, the film's points of view were also reduced to fragments in the wider sexuality curriculum.

Furthermore, given its focus at the level of classroom practice, the study illuminates the lived cultural responses of students as well as the tensions and contradictions related to gender, race, class, and sexual preference that are lived out there. Interview data also reveal numerous meanings behind this visible behavior. As summarized in the final section, students were shown to actively weigh their own interests in acquiescing to or contesting the film's points of view and classroom arrangements.

This analysis of the dynamics surrounding one presentation of media in a particular sexuality education classroom offers a picture of the complex, subtle, and sometimes contradictory process by which school knowledge is constructed. Several interconnected factors, including organizational imperatives of school and district as well as lived responses of students in the classroom, are involved in this process. Whatever the intended purpose or ideological message of educational media, it must work its way through these and other factors and may acquire alternate cultural meanings.

REFERENCES

Apple, M. W. (1979). *Ideology and curriculum*. London: Routledge & Kegan Paul.

Apple, M. W. (1982). *Education and power.* Boston: Routledge & Kegan Paul.

Bernstein, B. (1977). *Class, codes, and control: Towards a theory of educational transmissions* (Vol. III). London: Routledge & Kegan Paul.

Bourdieu, D., & Passeron, J. (1977). *Reproduction in education, society, and culture.* London: Sage.

Bowles, S., & Gintis, H. (1976). *Schooling in capitalist America.* New York: Basic Books.

Everhart, R. (1983). *Reading, writing, and resistance.* Boston: Routledge & Kegan Paul.

Lather, P. (1986). Issues of validity in openly ideological research: Between a rock and a soft place. *Interchange, 17* (4), 63–84.

McNeil, L. (1986). *Contradictions of control: School structure and school knowledge.* New York: Routledge & Kegan Paul.

New Dimension Films. (Producer). (1983a). *If you want to dance* [Film]. Eugene, OR.

New Dimension Films. (1983b). *If you want to dance* [Discussion guide]. Eugene, OR.

Orr, M. T. (1982). Sex education and contraceptive education in U.S. public high schools. *Family Planning Perspectives, 14* (6), 305–313.

Sonenstein, F. L., & Pittman, K. J. (1984). The availability of sex education in large city school districts. *Family Planning Perspectives, 16* (1), 19–25.

Trudell, B. (1988). *Constructing the sexuality curriculum-in-use: An ethnographic study of a ninth-grade school sex education class.* Unpublished doctoral dissertation, Curriculum and Instruction, School of Education, University of Wisconsin—Madison.

Valli, L. (1983). *Becoming clerical workers: An ethnographic study of office education and the social construction of work identity.* Ph.D. dissertation, Education Policy Studies, School of Education, University of Wisconsin—Madison.

Willis, P. (1977). *Marxism and literature.* Oxford: Oxford University Press.

6
Instructional Television Without Educators: The Beginning of ITV

ANN DE VANEY

Instructional television in elementary and secondary schools in the United States developed in the late 1950s in response to the launching of Sputnik and the crowding of classrooms. The decision to employ television as a vehicle for the delivery of math and science lessons was not made by professional educators, but by the congressional framers and administrators of the National Defense Education Act (NDEA). The decision to employ television to relieve crowded classrooms was not made by professional educators either, but by members of the boards of directors of the Ford Foundation agencies. These boards, consisting primarily of business executives and a few university administrators, sought to automate the classroom and selected television as the automaton to teach a mass audience of students. The Ford Foundation then contributed 90 percent of the television dollars spent on every elementary and secondary student in the United States between 1953 and 1963 (Finn, 1972; Saettler, 1968). This chapter will investigate the role played by the Ford Foundation agencies in the establishment of instructional television (ITV) during that innovative period.

In April 1952, the Federal Communications Commission (FCC) issued the Sixth Report and Order, which set aside 242 television channels (80 VHF and 162 UHF) for educational purposes. This was a momentous occasion that capped the intense lobbying efforts of a broad spectrum of petitioners, including university professors and deans, state and city school superintendents, public officials, teachers, and other educators (Saettler, 1968). During this period of burgeoning enrollments and severe teacher shortages, television was seen by many as a panacea for their educational ills and certainly for an educational system caught in a growth crisis. The positivist notion that technology will solve human problems has not disappeared from the field of education. It surfaces regularly with the introduction of new hardware. In the late 1960s mainframe computers were touted as the panacea for crowded classrooms and individualized instruction. Unfortunately microcomputers are currently viewed by some as a solution. But in the 1950s the feeling about the capability of television to reach a mass audience of students ran high.

With the new designation of channels, KUHT at the University of Houston rushed to air the first educational program on May 12, 1953. Some educators, however, were not novices in the design and production of instructional television. The University of Iowa had produced and narrowcast over 400 instructional programs on topics such as engineering, botany, art, drama, and shorthand between 1932 and 1939. Iowa State University, Kansas State University, the University of Michigan, and American University had also pioneered educational television (ETV) before 1952 (Powell, 1962). The Army and Navy had employed instructional television before this time and researched its structure and learning effects (Twyford & Seitz, 1956). I note these occurrences here because I wish to emphasize the fact that some expertise about the design and production of instructional television was available within the professions of education and instructional technology.

Within 10 years of the reservation of channels, only 63 financially troubled ETV stations were on the air (see Table 6.1), and by 1962 many expensive instructional television programs made for the classroom had been completely abandoned (Saettler, 1968). What happened to the hopes and the support of the broad spectrum of petitioners who believed in television as a means of instruction? Was it a simple awakening to the finite limitations of the vehicle, or were additional factors at play in the dismal representation of the medium? Whatever the answer, educators and instructional technologists, who know better, were blamed for the failure. In the late 1960s, ETV and ITV made a partial recovery because different lines of funding and design were pursued. The medium was not a complete flop: By 1968, an estimated 140 million people were watching ETV and over 15 million students viewed ITV in approximately 2000 schools (Powell, 1962).

Current accounts of the beginning of educational and instructional television in the 1950s cite the funding sources for their development, but fail to describe the profound influence these sources had on the design, production, and reception of television programs. Early ETV and ITV are often described in isolation without consideration of the milieu in which they emerged and without an account of the manner in which social and economic forces shaped the use of television in the classroom.

The 1950s was a decade of serious cold war with the Soviet Union and of national curricular revolution (Kliebard, 1986). It was also a time in which the balance of power over the operation of U.S. public schools was shifting away from teachers and professional educators to locales outside the schools. Yet, historians who recount the inception of ETV and ITV do not account for these forces. In fact, they are strangely dissimilar in their descriptions. In the 1960s, instructional technologists (Diamond, 1964; Saettler, 1968; Schramm, 1960) provided helpful case studies of early programs and highlighted the success of many of them, but they did not talk about the disappointment with or failures of the medium.

Some educational historians offer only a paragraph or two about ITV when describing the decade. And the Ford Foundation, which funded most of this innovation, has its own account of the period. The variance among these three narrative sources is remarkable, yet the goals of separate historical accounts might account for their differences. Instructional technologists, in an attempt to diffuse the innovations of teaching with television, concentrated on successful and appropriate applications of the medium. Educational historians may have considered early ITV a technological ripple that did not greatly affect the curriculum they wished to describe. These accounts are unelaborated and construct the development of ITV in an unproblematic manner. I do not mean to suggest that there are no authors who tackle the problem of the failure of early ITV, but those who do normally cite the cause as poor teacher training and teacher resistance, when indeed the seeds for failure had been sown in the television programs before they reached the classroom. Certainly, teachers were somewhat threatened by the new medium, but they were also smart enough to spot a program that would not teach. Larry Cuban (1986) discusses some of the problems of interface of television and the classroom in an insightful manner. There is a peculiar phenomenon at work here. Without conscious assent, it is as if the participants in this historic moment agreed to a partial collective amnesia about how and why the moment occurred.

This history is of interest today, not only because educators and instructional technologists were incorrectly blamed for the failure of ITV in that first decade (Becker, 1987), but for more important reasons. Tracing the sources of influence on the development of ITV allows practitioners, researchers, and designers to understand the medium not as a unique phenomenon, but as a predictable emergence of social and economic forces of that period. It also provides a means by which one may analyze the rhetoric of financial support for instructional television today and identify the manner in which the intentions of the funders are articulated in the development and production of video lessons.

Actually, the late 1980s and early 1990s bear a striking resemblance to the 1950s. There is rampant dissatisfaction with the way public schools are educating children, and a call for curricular reform has gone out

TABLE 6.1. Educational Television on the Air in 1961

State	Site	Station	Channel	On Air Date	FAE Grant
Alabama	Munford	WCIQ	7	1/55	
	Birmingham	WBIQ	10	4/55	
	University	WAIQ	2	8/56	X
Arizona	Tucson	KUAT	6	3/59	X
	Phoenix	KAET	8	1/61	
California	San Francisco	KQED	9	6/54	X
	Sacramento	KVIE	6	2/59	X
Colorado	Denver	KRMA	6	1/56	X
District of Columbia	Washington	WETA	26	10/61	
Florida	Miami	WTHS	2	8/55	X
	Jacksonville	WJCT	7	9/58	X
	Tampa-St. Petersburg	WEDU	3	10/58	
	Gainesville	WUFT	5	11/58	X
	Tallahassee	WFSU	11	9/60	
Georgia	Atlanta	WETA	30	2/58	X
	Athens	WGTV	8	9/55	X
	Waycross	WXGA	8	10/61	
Illinois	Champaign-Urbana	WILL	12	8/55	X
	Chicago	WTTW	11	9/55	X
	Carbondale	WSIU	8	9/61	
Iowa	Des Moines	KDPS	11	4/59	
Kentucky	Louisville	WFPK	15	9/58	
Louisiana	Monroe	KLSE	13	3/57	
	New Orleans	WYES	8	4/57	X
Maine	Augusta	WCBB	10	10/61	
Massachusetts	Boston	WGBH	2	5/55	X
Michigan	Detroit	WTVS	56	10/55	X
	Onondaga	WMSB	10	3/59	X
Missouri	St. Louis	KETC	9	9/54	X
	Kansas City	KCSD	19	3/61	
Nebraska	Lincoln	KUON	12	11/54	X
New Hampshire	Durham	WENH	11	7/59	X

TABLE 6.1. (Continued)

State	Site	Station	Channel	On Air Date	FAE Grant
New Mexico	Albuquerque	KNME	5	5/58	X
New York	Buffalo	WNED	17	3/59	
North Carolina	Chapel Hill	WUNC	4	1/55	X
Ohio	Cincinnati	WCET	48	7/54	X
	Columbus	WOSU	34	2/56	X
	Oxford	WMUB	14	10/59	
	Toledo	WGTE	30	1/60	
Oklahoma	Oklahoma City	KETA	13	4/56	
	Tulsa	KOED	11	1/59	
	Oklahoma City	KOKH	25	2/59	
Oregon	Corvallis	KOAC	7	10/57	
	Portland	KOAP	10	2/61	
Pennsylvania	Pittsburgh	WQED	13	4/54	X
	Philadelphia	WHYY	35	9/57	X
	Pittsburgh	WQEX	16	3/59	
Puerto Rico	San Juan	WIPR	6	1/58	
	Mayaguez	WIPM	3	3/61	
South Dakota	Vermillion	KUSD	2	7/61	
Tennessee	Memphis	WKNO	10	6/56	X
Texas	Houston	KUHT	8	5/53	
	Richardson	KRET	29	2/60	
	Dallas	KERA	13	9/60	X
Utah	Salt Lake City	KUED	7	1/58	X
	Ogden	KWCS	18	10/60	
Virginia	Norfolk-Hampton Roads	WHRO	15	10/61	
Washington	Seattle	KCTS	9	12/54	X
	Tacoma	KPEC	56	4/60	
	Tacoma	KTPS	62	9/61	
Wisconsin	Madison	WHA	21	3/54	X
	Milwaukee	WMVS	10	10/57	X

States with no educational television stations: Alaska, Arkansas, Delaware, Hawaii, Idaho, Indiana, Kansas, Maryland, Mississippi, Montana, Nevada, New Jersey, North Dakota, Rhode Island, South Carolina, Vermont, West Virginia, Wyoming

Source: Channels of Learning, by J. W. Powell, 1967, Washington, DC: Public Affairs Press.

across the country. Like the directives of the 1950s, recent demands have been for a return to classical education (Bloom, 1987; Hirsch, 1987). Current educators, unlike those in the 1950s, are not turning to television as a panacea. In fact, television has lost much status as a teacher, but many are turning to microcomputers. The Federal Register again stresses the importance of "mathematics, science and relevant foreign languages" in its daily calls for educational research proposals. That exact language was used in the requests for proposals under the NDEA of 1958 (Sufrin, 1963). Many professional educators are being bypassed again. With the current teacher shortage, which is a product of the baby boomlet, some municipal school districts are hiring uncredentialed teachers and electing to teach and offer credentials themselves, rather than let their prospective teachers be tainted by schools of education. In many ways the current climate reproduces some of the social conditions of the 1950s.

It is not only the similarity of the two periods that makes investigating the early years of ITV intriguing, but the fact that if educators are to understand how the medium is constituted today, they must understand how it began. Since the Ford Foundation indirectly created much of this early history, we will investigate that agency's contribution. The Ford Foundation provided 90% of the television dollars spent on each elementary and secondary student between 1953 and 1963. If the foundation had an agenda and if that agenda was carried out, its facilitators controlled 90% of the television programming reaching elementary and secondary classrooms. Questions of interest are, "What was that agenda, and who were these facilitators?"

BACKGROUND

An accepted distinction between ITV and ETV is that instructional television consists of telecourses designed for credit, and educational television creates informational and aesthetic programs for general viewing. The distinction was often blurred during the 1950s and became blurred again in the late 1980s, when the Public Broadcasting System (PBS) reentered the instructional market by producing and airing courses for credit. This current shift was prompted by the flagging finances of PBS stations. The Annenberg Foundation, much like the Ford Foundation in the 1950s, has proffered life-saving grants, which are helping to keep public television stations afloat. Instruction for credit, rather than general educational programming, is the goal of the Annenberg Foundation. In fact, the Annenberg Foundation board members would like to see junior college courses delivered to all U.S. homes by the mid-1990s, and it is to that end that they have pledged large sums of money over a 10-year period.

The Ford Foundation had similar high ambitions for U.S. students in the 1950s, and over a 10-year period poured $143.3 million into educational and instructional television. The primary channels through which these monies were filtered were the Fund for the Advancement of Education (FAE), the National Educational Television and Radio Center (NET), and the Public Broadcast Laboratory (Nagal, 1979). Before the outcome of the foundation's massive effort is described, its goals will be examined. What was it they hoped to accomplish?

THE FORD FOUNDATION

The Ford Foundation is an outstanding philanthropic, tax-free, non-profit organization that has spent billions of dollars since its inception in 1936 to promote peace, international development, education, and social progress (Magat, 1979). It should be understood that the current structure of PBS is due, in large part, to the financial support of the foundation during the decade in question. The foundation, however, through the Fund for Advancement of Education, had an agenda for the U.S. public schools in the 1950s and early 1960s. (Table 6.1 indicates that half of the ETV stations on the air in 1961 had been initiated and supported by FAE monies.) Not every funding agency pursues so explicit an agenda. Prior to the 1950s educational support for classroom audiovisual aids came primarily from the Rockefeller Foundation and the Payne Fund. Grants from these sources were awarded directly to educators, who were free to implement the money within the existing structure of the schools. That was not the case with the Ford money (Finn, 1972; Saettler, 1968).

To settle the educational crisis of the 1950s, namely, a rapidly growing student population, the Fund for the Advancement of Education, which was the Ford Foundation's conduit to elementary and secondary classrooms and distributed most of the Ford television money, wished to automate the classroom. More specifically, FAE board members wished to automate the classroom (Finn, 1972). An examination of the Ford Foundation's Annual Reports (1951–57) reveals that the board officers and trustees were successful corporate businesspeople who headed banks, newspapers, and factories; attorneys (there was even one judge); and a college president. There was not one public school administrator, teacher, professor of education, or instructional technologist on this board. That was also true of all the other funding boards through which the Ford Foundation filtered its money for the development of ETV and

ITV. The one exception to this was the Joint Council on Educational Television Committee on Television, American Council on Education, which received the smallest grants sporadically over the ten years in question (Ford Foundation's Annual Reports, 1951–57). The board of the Fund for Advancement of Education consisted of two business executives plus the president of Encyclopaedia Britannica Films, an editorial writer, a former radio scriptwriter, and a film producer. The National Educational Television and Radio Center fared only a bit better. Its organizing committee consisted of two college presidents, one law professor, one business executive, and two research institute presidents (Saettler, 1968). Even though college presidents may be thought of as professional educators, they usually do not have pedagogical training, but ascend to their positions through departments in the schools of letters and science, and usually have no familiarity with elementary and secondary education.

The bypassing of elementary and secondary professional educators and instructional technologists cannot be considered in isolation and was not unusual for the time. Large segments of the private sector had coalesced in an attack on U.S. schools (Bestor, 1953), and professional educators were the scapegoats for the populace. There was a general feeling that private citizens wished to take things into their own hands and directly influence curriculum. As noted above, similar sentiment exists today.

Two board members who described the intentions of the FAE were Alexander Stoddard and Alvin Eurich. In various documents (Finn, 1972), they stated that the Fund's principal concern was with the impending shortage of teachers. They believed that the solution to the crisis in education (growing student population) must come from automating the teaching process. "In television," Eurich wrote, "we now have available an almost perfect educational instrument" (1956, p. 10). Television, they thought, could make it feasible for a few good instructors to reach and influence large numbers of students. They were certainly not considering employing existing elementary or secondary teachers, who they thought were doing such a poor job in the classrooms of the 1950s. They indicated that the Fund wanted whole courses taught by television to "substitute for and lessen what the regular teacher must do" (Stoddard, 1957, p. 43) and achieve a high level of teaching efficiency with fewer trained teachers. Finn (1972) summarizes the intentions of the FAE board members. He notes that they wished to leave all aspects of teaching and pedagogy to transmitted programs, and supervisory aspects to persons in the classroom; to develop a group of master teachers who would prepare and deliver the transmitted lessons; and to raise the quality of teaching because these master teachers would be experts who possessed specialized knowledge not available to line teachers. The board members' no-

TABLE 6.2. Estimate of Ford Foundation ITV Expenditures

Fund/Function	Expenditure ($ millions)	Years
Fund for Advancement of Education	47.4	1951–1961
Radio and Television Workshop	8.0	1951–1957
Release time for Letters and Science faculty	1.8	1956–1961
ITV program production	11.7	1951–1960
Construction of ETV stations	4.0	1959–1962
Midwest Program on Airborne Television	14.7	1959–1962
Public Broadcast Laboratory	12.0	1951–1957

tion of automation was not limited to school districts or even states. Eurich (1956) believed that instructional television programs might as well be transmitted on a national level.

The Ford Foundation devoted substantial amounts of money to the pursuit of its educational agenda. It is difficult to estimate the actual expenditure because reports conflict and often fail to break down aggregate figures, but the figures presented in Table 6.2, derived from Magat (1979), provide a reasonable overview of the foundation's ITV disbursements in the 1950s and early 1960s. The impressive total—nearly $100 million—made the foundation a preeminent force in shaping instructional broadcasting.

HISTORICAL PRECEDENT

What this enormous outlay of Ford Foundation money represented during the years 1953 to 1963 was the start of public television broadcasting and the source of 90 percent of the television programs delivered to U.S. classrooms. But these early instructional television programs failed, and the foundation withdrew its money from the debacle in 1963. This effort was a precedent-setting event in the history of U.S. education.

Prior to the 1950s neither the federal government nor any private corporation had set broad agendas for schools across the country. The federal government had supported vocational education, among other things, but passage of the NDEA represented the first massive intervention on the part of the federal government to restructure curriculum. A shift in the locus of control of the curriculum from educators to academics was envisioned by the framers of this act. National centers for the design and dissemination of public school curriculum were created with NDEA money, and professors of letters and science were hired to generate national curriculum. This national model ran counter to prior models of curriculum development, which traditionally had been local (Kliebard, 1986). It is not surprising then that, concurrently, the Ford Foundation attempted to effect a national curriculum through instructional television. This signalled a convergence of political and social forces at the national level.

A widespread misconception about the passage of the NDEA and the start of instructional television in the schools is that they occurred solely because of the launching of Sputnik and the crowding of classrooms. But larger social forces were at work. In the early 1950s, the public schools were solidly under the influence of a practical life curriculum. A "life adjustment" curriculum, legitimated by the 1945 Prosser Resolution, was the dominant educational model (Kliebard, 1986). Such a model sought to "democratize" education and help prepare average citizens for practical careers. In the late 1940s and early 1950s, the federal government sided with educators and financially supported vocational education. But there was a growing concern about the perceived inability of educators to prepare students in the "basics"—reading, writing, and math. Arthur Bestor (1953) led the attack against the schools with *Educational Wastelands: The Retreat from Learning in Our Public Schools* (reissued in 1985 by the University of Illinois Press), and many other critics followed suit. Their argument was that the "life adjustment" curriculum was anti-intellectual and, since it tracked students, was actually anti-democratic. Constituents addressed fears about their children's education to their congresspeople, and a massive "back to basics" movement was underway (Kliebard, 1986). The launching of Sputnik provided additional impetus to this movement.

ITV PRODUCTION MODELS

Educators were bypassed since the public thought they had failed to educate children in the "basics." Their support of practical life education was cited as the cause, but the Ford Foundation board members had another knowledgeable resource that they could have tapped—educational film producers. Relying on instructional film research of World War II and their experience in the U.S. public schools since the 1920s, educational film producers had developed models of potentially successful film design. In the 1950s, their favorite format was dramatic narrative (Ellsworth, 1987), which engaged student viewers by means of identification. They had learned from research during World War II that using a lecture and a talking head in a motion medium was deadly and the least effective way to deliver information. But educational film was entrenched in the schools, and the practices of a host of powerful producers (Coronet,

Oxford, McGraw-Hill, International Films, and so on) had become institutionalized. After World War II, educators, instructional technologists, and Hollywood film producers participated in the educational film enterprise. They acted variously as consultants, designers, scriptwriters, and producers, and thus formed the infrastructure of the educational film industry. It would have been difficult for Ford board members to mandate changes in the production models of these educational media experts. Also, classroom films of this period responded to the needs of the life adjustment curriculum and came under the fire of Arthur Bestor (1953) and other critics. Films such as *Your Family, Magic Food, The ABCs of Walking Wisely, Social Sex Attitudes, The Dangerous Stranger, A Day at the Fair,* and other practical presentations were critiqued for their nonscholarly content. The important point of the criticism is that these films were the only ones being produced. They were not balanced by films on academic topics (Ellsworth, 1987). Film, which is now perceived as more serious and artistic than television, was then considered nonintellectual by early ITV developers.

Another anomaly that accompanied the start of ITV was its unusual incorporation of production practices. Marshall McLuhan (1964) points out that the products of a new medium whose unique capabilities are unknown are simple imitations of prior similar media. Early Hollywood cinema imitated dime romance and western novels because their plots were similar. Early broadcast television imitated Hollywood cinema and because of stationary cameras, legitimate theater. But early ITV inclined itself toward failure by imitating the practices of domains quite dissimilar to its own. Since broadcast radio stations were folding in the early 1950s, radio producers were often hired by new educational television stations (Powell, 1962). These transferees, accustomed to a nonvisual medium, emphasized the audio track of this highly visual medium, and radio production conventions became incorporated in the new ITV. Likewise, the selection of an ITV format was influenced by an unusual form of communication, the college lecture.

Educators, educational technologists, and educational film makers were discredited by their participation in the dominant life adjustment curriculum of the 1950s. Ford Foundation board members, as did the administrators of the NDEA, turned away from educators and toward subject-matter experts. They hired only professors from colleges of Letters and Science, who, without training in instructional methods or audiovisual design, designed, scripted, and acted in early instructional television programs. They turned to the only format with which they were familiar, the lecture. Both the Ford Foundation and the universities from which these experts were drawn considered this work as intellectual activity that would deliver lessons to U.S. schools and advance the personal careers of those faculty involved. To that end the Ford Foundation contributed $1.8 million for faculty release time from 1956 to 1961, and deans released faculty members for one year to pursue their academic careers. When the members of the board of the FAE realized that these experts were not teaching, they halted the release program.

A stationary and stilted format became the format of choice for a new visually dynamic educational medium. Lecture, which is predominantly a talking head, encodes specific meanings. The participants in this early enterprise probably considered television a neutral transparent medium, a window on the world, and did not account for the manner in which television transforms an authentic event and tells its own story. Communicative codes inherent in classroom lectures become somewhat exaggerated on the television screen. Whether a talking head is used in film or television, it suggests that the person talking is the authority, an expert who is imparting knowledge to novices. This view coincided with the intentions of the FAE board members and the administrators of the NDEA, but lecture inscribes a restricted form of pedagogy. The voice of authority emphasizes the hierarchical nature of the classroom and employs the banking concept of teaching, which occurs when an instructor simply deposits facts in the minds of pupils and waits for them to make a withdrawal. These early ITV programs were jammed with facts in the audio track and little motion or visual aids in the video track.

As noted above, the opportunity existed to imitate film practices or to learn from the research on instructional film and television, which had been completed by the mid-1950s. In a joint report for the Army and the Navy, Twyford and Seitz (1956) warned about the use of the talking head on television. Speeches, they indicated, were usually too long and detracted from the instructional value of a program. They offered ITV design guidelines, drawn from television, for format, screen size, production, and learning.

The talking head is employed less frequently in today's ITV programs, but its legacy persists in a new manner. Instead of employing the ineffective lecture format, today's designers often use voice-over by an off-camera narrator to describe what is happening in the visual track. In media studies, this is called the "voice of God" and again offers viewers the hierarchical pedagogy.

WHY FAILURE?

For almost 10 years, powerful citizens in the private sector who sat on Ford Foundation boards decided what specific curriculums would be delivered to U.S. classrooms and how they would be delivered. Moreover, their decisions to a large extent set the course for the public sector, for while the Ford Foundation supplied most of the software for television courses, much of the hardware was supplied to schools by monies from the NDEA. Yet despite the millions of dollars poured in from both sources, these massive efforts inevitably failed because elemental mistakes had been made from the outset:

A stilted format was selected for a dynamic medium.
A hierarchical pedagogy that stifled participation was employed.
Faculty untrained in instructional media and curriculum design were chosen to design, script, and act in the ITV programs.
Programs designed for national distribution ignored the conventions of local curriculum design.

It would be hopeful but presumptuous to say that a lesson had been learned from the failure of early ITV. Contrary to positivist notions, the passage of time does not indicate progress. In fact, a scenario similar to the 1950s is currently unfolding. As noted above, present-day educators and schools have again become the scapegoats for students' social problems. Private sector interest in the curriculum grows daily and expresses itself in programs such as Channel One, CNN Newsroom, and the plethora of ITV courses sponsored by the Annenberg Foundation. And, as before, educators' input into these programs is practically nonexistent and subject matter consultants are drawn from colleges of Letters and Science. The ITV project seems destined to repeat itself in a technically more sophisticated fashion. Adding fuel to the fire are the misperceptions that have been promulgated about the failure of early ITV. As noted above, teacher resistance received the blame and the causes described in this chapter remain publicly unarticulated.

REFERENCES

Becker, A. (1987). Instructional television and the talking head. *Education Technology, 27*, 35–40.

Bestor, A. (1953). *Educational wastelands: The retreat from learning in our public schools*. Urbana: University of Illinois Press. (Reissued 1985).

Bloom, A. D. (1987). *The closing of the American mind*. New York: Simon & Schuster.

Cuban, Larry. (1986). *Teachers and machines: The classroom use of technology since 1920*. New York: Teachers College Press.

Diamond, R. M. (Ed.). (1964). *A Guide to Instructional Television*. New York: McGraw-Hill.

Eurich, A. (1956). Better instruction with fewer teachers. *Current Issues in Higher Education*. Washington, DC: Association for Higher Education, NEA, 10–16.

Ellsworth, E. (1987). Fiction as proof: Critical analysis of the form, style, and ideology of educational dramatization films. *Proceedings of selected research paper presentations at the 1987 AECT Convention sponsored by the Research and Theory Division*. Atlanta.

Finn, J. (1972). Automatizing the classroom: Background of the effort. In R. Mcbeath (Ed.), *Extending education through technology* (pp. 125–139). Washington, DC: Association for Educational Communications and Technology.

Ford Foundation. (1951). *The Ford Foundation annual report for 1951*. Dearborn, MI: Author.

Ford Foundation. (1952). *The Ford Foundation annual report for 1952*. Dearborn, MI: Author.

Ford Foundation. (1953). *The Ford Foundation annual report for 1953*. Dearborn, MI: Author.

Ford Foundation. (1954). *The Ford Foundation annual report 1954: To advance human welfare*. Dearborn, MI: Author.

Ford Foundation. (1955). *The Ford Foundation annual report 1955: To advance human welfare*. Dearborn, MI: Author.

Ford Foundation. (1956). *The Ford Foundation annual report 1956*. Dearborn, MI: Author.

Ford Foundation. (1957). *The Ford Foundation annual report 1957*. Dearborn, MI: Author.

Hirsch, E. D. (1987). *Cultural literacy: What every American needs to know*. Boston: Houghton Mifflin.

Kliebard, H. (1986). *The struggle for the American curriculum 1893–1958*. Boston: Routledge & Kegan Paul.

McLuhan, Marshall. (1964). *Understanding media: The extensions of man*. New York: McGraw-Hill.

Magat, R. (1979). *The Ford Foundation at work: Philanthropic choices, methods and styles*. New York: Plenum Press.

Powell, J. W. (1962). *Channels of learning*. Washington, DC: Public Affairs Press.

Saettler, P. (1968). *A history of instructional technology*. New York: McGraw-Hill.

Schramm, W. (Ed.). (1960). *The impact of educational television*. Urbana: University of Illinois Press.

Stoddard, A. (1957). *Schools for tomorrow: An educator's blueprint*. New York: Fund for the Advancement of Education.

Sufrin, S. C. (1963). *Administering the National Defense Education Act*. Syracuse, NY: Syracuse University Press.

Twyford, L., & Seitz, C. (1956). *Instructional television research reports*. Port Washington, NY: U.S. Naval Training Center.

7
The Picture of Health: How Textbook Photographs Construct Health

MARIAMNE H. WHATLEY

Photographs in textbooks may serve the roles of breaking up a long text, emphasizing or clarifying information in the text, attracting the buyer (the professor, teacher, or administrator who selects texts), and engaging the reader. But photographs cannot be dismissed merely as either decorative additions or straightforward illustrations of the text. Photographs are often far more memorable than the passages they illustrate and, because they are seen as objective representations of reality, rather than artists' constructions (Barthes, 1977), may have more impact than drawings or other forms of artwork. In textbooks, photographs can carry connotations, intentional or not, never stated in the text. The selection of photographs for a text is not a neutral process that simply involves being "realistic" or "objective"; selection must take into account issues such as audience expectations and dominant meanings in a given cultural/ historical context (Whatley, 1988). In order to understand the ideological work of a textbook, a critique of the photographs is as crucial as a critique of the text itself.

Using ideological analysis to identify patterns of inclusion and exclusion, I examined photographs in the seven best-selling, college-level personal health textbooks. This chapter presents the results of that research. In the first part of the analysis, I examined the photographs that represent "health," describing who and what is "healthy," according to these representations. In the second part of the analysis, I determined where those excluded from the definition of health are represented in the approximately 1,100 remaining photographs in the texts.

SELLING HEALTH IN TEXTBOOKS

Generally, textbook authors do not select specific photographs but may give publishers general descriptions of the type of photographs they wish to have included (for example, a scene showing urban crowding, a woman in a nontraditional job). Due to the great expense involved, new photographs are not usually taken specifically for texts. Instead publishers hire photo researchers to find appropriate photographs, drawing on already existing photographic collections. The result is that the choice of photographs depends on what is already available, and what is available depends to some extent on what has been requested in the past. In fact, because the same sources of photographs may be used by a number of different publishers, identical photographs may appear in competing books. Although authors may have visions of their books' "artwork," the reality may be limited by the selection already on the market. In addition, editors and publishers make decisions about what "artwork" will sell or is considered appropriate, sometimes overruling the authors' choices.

Photographs, especially cover-photos and special color sections, are considered features that sell textbooks, but they also can work as part of another selling process. Textbooks, in many cases, sell the reader a system of belief. An economics text, for example, may "sell" capitalism, and a science text may "sell" the scientific method, both of which help support dominant ideologies. Health textbooks may be even more invested in this selling process because, in addition to convincing readers to "believe" in health, their "success" depends on the readers' adoption of very specific personal behavioral programs to attain health. Health textbooks hold up the ideals of "total wellness" or "holistic fitness" as goals we can attain by exercising, eating right, reducing stress, and avoiding drugs. The readers' belief in health and their ability to attain it by specific behaviors is seen by many health educators as necessary to relevant educational goals; the belief in a clearly marked pathway to health is also part of a process of the commodification of health.

In North America and Western Europe, health is currently a very marketable commodity. This can be seen in its most exaggerated form in the United States in the proliferation of "health" clubs, in the trend among hospitals and clinics to attract a healthy clientele by advertising their abilities to make healthy people healthier (Worcester & Whatley, 1988), and in the advertisements that link a wide range of products, such as high fiber cereals and calcium rich antacids, to health. In a recent article in a medical journal, a physician examined this commercialization of health:

> Health is industrialized and commercialized in a fashion that enhances many people's dissatisfaction with their health. Advertisers, manufacturers, advocacy groups, and proprietary health care corporations promote the myth that

good health can be purchased; they market products and services that purport to deliver the consumer into the promised land of wellness. (Barsky, 1988, p. 415)

Photographs in health textbooks can play a role in this selling of health similar to that played by visual images in advertising a product in the popular media. According to Berger (1972), the role of advertising or publicity is to

make the spectator marginally dissatisfied with his present way of life. Not with the way of life of society, but with his own place within it. It suggests that if he buys what it is offering, his life will become better. It offers him an improved alternative to what he is. (p. 142)

The ideal of the healthy person and the healthy lifestyle can be seen as the "improved alternative" to what we are. It can be assumed that most of us will be dissatisfied with ourselves when measured against that ideal, just as most women are dissatisfied with their body shapes and sizes when compared with ideal media representations.

In effective advertising campaigns the visual image is designed to provoke powerful audience responses. In health textbooks the visual representation of "health" is calculated to sell, and it is likely to have a greater impact on the reader than discussions about lengthened life expectancy, reduction in chronic illness, or enhanced cardiovascular fitness. The image of health, not health itself, may be what most people strive for. In the attempt to look healthy, many sacrifice health. For example, people go through very unhealthy practices to lose "extra" weight that is in itself not unhealthy; being slim, however, is a basic component of the *appearance* of health. A recent survey found that people who eat healthy foods do so for their appearance and *not* for their health. "Tanning parlors" have become common features of health and fitness centers, though tanning in itself is unhealthy. As with being slim, having a good tan contributes to the appearance of what is currently defined as health.

The use of color photographs is particularly effective in selling the healthy image, for, as Berger (1972) points out, both oil painting and color photography "use similar highly tactile means to play upon the spectator's sense of acquiring the *real* thing which the image shows" (p. 141). The recent improvement in quality and the increase in number of color photographs in textbooks provide an opportunity to sell the image of health even more effectively than black and white photographs could.

SELECTION OF TEXTBOOKS

Rather than trying to examine all college-level personal health (as opposed to community health) textbooks, I selected the best-selling ones, since those would have the widest impact. Based on the sales figures provided by the publisher of one popular text, I selected seven texts published from 1985 to 1988. Sales of these textbooks ranged from approximately 15,000 to 50,000 for each edition. (Complete bibliographic information on these textbooks is provided in the Appendix. Author-date citations to these textbooks refer to the Appendix, rather than the chapter references.) Obviously, the sales figures depend on the number of years a specific edition has been in print. For one text (Insel & Roth, 1988), I examined the newest edition (for which there could be no sales figures), based on the fact that its previous editions had high sales. A paper on the readability of personal health textbooks (Overman, Mimms, & Harris, 1987), using a similar selection process, examined the seven top-selling textbooks for the 1984–85 school year, plus three other random titles. Their list has an overlap with mine of only four texts, which may be due to a number of factors, including differences in editions and changing sales figures.

ANALYSIS I: HEALTHY–IMAGE PHOTOGRAPHS

The first step in my analysis was a close examination of the photographs that I saw as representing "health," the images intended to show who is healthy and illustrate the healthy lifestyle. These included photographs used on covers, opposite title pages, and as openers to units or chapters on wellness or health (as opposed to specific topics such as nutrition, drugs, and mental health). While other pictures throughout the texts may represent healthy individuals, the ones selected, by their placement in conjunction with the book title or chapter title, can be seen as clearly connoting "health." I will refer to these as healthy-image photographs. I included in this analysis only photographs in which there were people. While an apple on a cover conveys a message about health, I was interested only in the question of who is healthy.

A total of 18 different photographs fit my criteria for representing health. I have eliminated three of these from discussion: the cover from Insel and Roth (1988) showing flowers and, from Dintiman and Greenberg (1986), both the cover photograph of apples and the health unit opener of a movie still from the *Wizard of Oz*. (This textbook uses movie stills as openers for all chapters; this moves the photograph away from its perceived "objective" status toward that of an obvious construction.)

There are a number of points of similarity in the 15 remaining photographs. In several photographs (windsurfing, hang gliding), it is hard to determine race, but all individuals whose faces can clearly be seen are white. Except for those who cannot be seen clearly and for several of the eight skydivers in a health unit opener, all are young. No one in these photographs is fat or has any identifiable physical disability. Sports dominate the activities, which, with the exception of rhythmic gymnastics and volleyball played in a gym, are outdoor activities in nonurban settings. Five of these involve beaches or open water. All the activities are leisure activities, with no evidence of work. While it is impossible to say anything definitive about class from these photographs, several of the activities are expensive (hang gliding, skydiving, windsurfing), and others may take money and/or sufficient time off from work to get to places where they can be done (beaches, biking in countryside); these suggest middle-class activities, whether the actual individuals are middle class or not. In several photographs (windsurfing, hang gliding, swimming) it is hard to determine gender. However, excluding these and the large group of male runners in a cross-country race, the overall balance is 23 males to 18 females, so it does seem that there is an attempt to show women both as healthy individuals and in active roles.

How Health Is Portrayed

A detailed analysis of three photographs can provide insight into how these text photographs construct health. The first is a color photograph of a volleyball game on a beach from the back cover of *Understanding Your Health* (Payne & Hahn, 1986). As with most of these images of health, the setting is outdoors, clearly at a distance from urban life. The steep rock walls that serve as a backdrop to the volleyball game additionally isolate the natural beach setting from the invasion of cars[1] and other symbols of "man-made" environmental destruction and ill health. The volleyball players appear to have escaped into a protected idyllic setting of sun, sand, and, we assume, water. They also have clearly escaped from work, since they are engaged in a common leisure activity associated with picnics and holidays. None of them appears to be contemplating the beauty of the natural setting, but merely using it as a location for a game that could go on anywhere in which there is room to set up a net.

The photograph is framed in such a way that the whole net and area of the "court" are not included, so that some players may also not be visible. On one side of the net are three women and a man, on the other two women and a man. While this is not necessarily a representation of heterosexual interactions, it can be read that way. Two players are the focus of the picture, with the other five essentially out of the action. The woman who has just hit the ball, with her back toward the camera, has her arms outstretched, her legs slightly spread, and one foot partly off the ground. The man who is waiting for the ball is crouched slightly, looking expectantly upward. Her body is partially superimposed on his, her leg crossed over his. This is essentially an interaction between one man and one woman. It would not work the same way if the key players were both female or both male, since part of the "healthiness" of this image appears to be the heterosexual interaction. For heterosexual men, this scene might be viewed as ideal—a great male-female ratio on an isolated beach; perhaps this is their reward for having arrived at the end of this book—this photograph is on the *back* cover—attaining their goal of health.

All the volleyball players are white, young, and slim. The woman farthest left in the frame appears slightly heavier than the others; she is the only woman wearing a shirt, rather than a bikini top, and is also wearing shorts. Besides being an outsider in terms of weight, dress, and location in the frame, she is the only woman who clearly has short hair (three have long hair tied back in ponytails, one cannot be seen completely). Perhaps she can move "inside" by losing weight and changing her image. As viewers, we are just a few steps beyond the end of the court and are also outsiders. As with pick-up games, there is room for observers to enter the game—if they are deemed acceptable by the other players. By achieving health, perhaps the observer can step into the game, among the young, white, slim, heterosexual, and physically active. But if the definition of health includes young, white, slim, heterosexual, and physically active, many observers are relegated permanently to the outside.

If this photograph serves as an invitation to join in the lifestyle of the young and healthy, the second photograph, facing the title page of another book, serves the same function, with the additional written message provided by the title of the book—*An Invitation to Health* (Hales & Williams, 1986). The photograph is of six bicycle riders, three women and three men, resting astride their bicycles. This photograph is in black and white, so it is perhaps not as seductive as the sunny color of the first cover. However, the people in this photograph are all smiling directly at the viewer (rather than just leaving a space in back where the viewer could join in). Two of the women, in the middle and the right, have poses and smiles that could be described as flirtatious. They are taking a break from their riding, so it is an opportune moment to join the fun of being healthy.

As with the volleyball players, all the bicycle riders are young, slim, white, and apparently fit. Another similarity is the amount of skin that is exposed. Playing volleyball on the beach and riding bikes in warm weather are activities for which shorts and short-sleeved shirts are preferable to sweatpants and sweatshirts. The choice of these types of activities to represent health results in photographs in which legs and arms are not covered. Appearing healthy apparently involves no need to cover up unsightly flab, "cellulite," or stretch marks. A healthy body is a body that can be revealed.

The bikers are in a fairly isolated, rural setting. While they are clearly on the road, it appears to be a rural, relatively untraveled road. Two cars can be seen far in the distance, and there may also be a house in the distance on the right side of the frame. Otherwise, the landscape is dominated by hills, trees, and grass. The setting and the activity clearly distance the bike riders both from urban life and from work.

In a third photograph, a health unit chapter opener (Levy, Dignan, & Shirreffs, 1987), we can see a possible beginning to alternative images of health. The players in this volleyball game are still slim, young, and apparently white. However, the setting is a gym, which could be urban, suburban, or rural. While four of the players are wearing shorts, one woman is wearing sweatpants; there are T-shirts rather than bikini tops, and gym socks rather than bare legs. The impression is that they are there to play a hard game of volleyball rather than to bask in the sun and each other's gaze. Two men are going for the ball from opposite sides, while a woman facing the net is clearly ready to move. Compared with the other volleyball scene, this photograph gives more of a sense of action, of actual physical exertion, as well as a sense of real people, rather than models.

It is interesting to imagine how healthy the volleyball players and bike riders actually are, underneath the appearance of health. The outdoor groups, especially the beach group, are susceptible to skin cancer from overexposure to the sun. Cycling is a healthy aerobic sport, though it can be hard on the knees and back. It is particularly surprising, however, to find that the bikers represented in a health text are not wearing helmets, thus modelling behavior that is considered very risky. Compared with biking, volleyball is the kind of weekend activity that sends the enthusiastic untrained player home with pulled muscles, jammed fingers, and not much of a useful workout. The question also arises as to how the particularly thin women on the beach achieved their weight—

by unhealthy weight-loss diets, by anorexia, by purging? The glowing image of health may have little to do with the reality.

Similarities to Advertising

Shortly after I began the research for this chapter, I was startled, while waiting for a movie to begin, to see a soft drink advertisement from which almost any still could have been substituted for a healthy-image photograph I had examined. There were the same thin, young, white men and women frolicking on the beach, playing volleyball, and wind-surfing. They were clearly occupying the same territory: a never-never land of eternal sunshine, eternal youth, and eternal leisure. Given my argument that these textbook photographs are selling health, the similarities between soft drink advertising images and textbook healthy images are not surprising. They are appealing to the same groups of people, and they are both attempting to create an association between a desirable lifestyle and their product. You can enjoy this fun in the sun if you are part of the "Pepsi generation" or think "Coke is it" or follow the textbook's path to health. These can be considered one variant of the lifestyle format in advertising, as described by Leiss, Kline, and Jhally (1986).

> Here the activity invoked in text or image becomes the central cue for relating the person, product, and setting codes. Lifestyle ads commonly depict a variety of leisure activities (entertaining, going out, holidaying, relaxing). Implicit in each of these activities, however, is the placing of the product within a consumption style by its link to an activity. (p. 210)

Even a naive critic of advertising could point out that drinking a carbonated beverage could not possibly help anyone attain this lifestyle; on the other hand, it might be easier to accept that the same lifestyle is a result of achieving health. However, the association between health and this leisure lifestyle is as much a construction as that created in the soft drink ads. Following all the advice in these textbooks as to diet, exercise, coping with stress, and attaining a healthy sexuality will not help anyone achieve this sun-and-fun fantasy lifestyle any more than drinking Coke or Pepsi would.

These healthy-image photographs borrow directly from popular images of ideal lifestyles already very familiar to viewers through advertising[2] and clearly reflect the current marketing of health. The result is that health is being sold with as much connection to real life and real people's needs as liquor ads that suggest major lifestyle changes associated with changing one's brand of scotch.

ANALYSIS II: WHERE ARE THE EXCLUDED?

For each textbook, the next step was to write brief descriptions of all other photographs in the books, totaling approximately 1,100. The results of the analysis of the healthy-image photographs suggested a focus on specific aspects of the description of the individuals and activities in examining the remaining 1,100 photographs. The areas I selected for discussion are those in which "health" is linked to specific lifestyles or factors that determine social position/power in our society. I described the setting, the activity, and a number of observable points about the people, including gender, race, age, physical ability/disability, and weight. These photographs were all listed by chapter and, when appropriate, by particular topic in that chapter. For example, a chapter on mental health might have images of positive mental health and also images representing problems such as severe depression or stress. These descriptions of photographs were used to establish whether there were images with characteristics not found in the healthy images and, if so, the context in which these characteristics were present. For example, finding no urban representations among the healthy images, I identified topic headings under which I did find photographs of urban settings.

White, young, thin, physically abled, middle-class people in the healthy images represent the mythical norm with whom the audience is supposed to identify. This not only creates difficulties in identification for those who do not meet these criteria, but also creates a limiting and limited definition of health. I examined the photographs that did not fit the healthy-image definition to find the invisible—those absent from the healthy images: people of color, people with physical disabilities, fat people, and old people. I also attempted to identify two other absences—the urban setting and work environment. Because there were no obvious gender discrepancies in the healthy images, I did not examine gender as a separate category.

People of Color

After going through the remaining photographs, it was clear that there had been an attempt to include photographs of people of color in a variety of settings, but no obvious patterns emerged. In a previous paper, I examined representations of African-Americans in sexuality texts, finding that positive attempts at being nonracist could be undermined by the patterns of photographs in textbooks that, for example, draw on stereotypes and myths of "dangerous" black sexuality (Whatley, 1988). Rather than reviewing all the representations of people of color in these health textbooks, I will simply repeat what I pointed out earlier—that there is a strong and clear *absence* of photographs of people of color in the healthy-images category. People of color may appear as healthy people elsewhere in the text, but not on covers, title pages, and chapter openers. If publishers wanted to correct this situation, they could simply substitute group photographs that show some diversity for the current all-white covers and title pages.

People with Disabilities

From the healthy-image photographs, it is apparent that people with visible physical disabilities are excluded from the definition of healthy. Therefore, I examined the contexts in which people with disabilities appear in the other photographs. Out of the approximately 1,100 photos, only 9 show people with physical disabilities, with 2 of these showing isolated body parts only (arthritic hands and knees). One shows an old woman being pushed in a wheelchair, while the six remaining photographs all are "positive" images: a number of men playing wheelchair basketball, a man in a wheelchair doing carpentry, a woman walking with her arm around a man in a wheelchair, a man with an amputated leg walking across Canada, children with cancer (which can be seen both as a disease and a disability) at a camp (these last two both in a cancer chapter), and a wheelchair racer. However, three of these six are from one textbook (Payne & Hahn, 1986), and two are from another (Levy, Dignan, & Shirreffs, 1987), so the inclusion of these few positive images is overshadowed by the fact that three books show absolutely none. In addition, none of these positive images are of women, and the only disabilities represented are those in which an individual uses a wheelchair or has cancer.

This absence of representation of disabled people, particularly women, clearly reflects the invisibility of the physically disabled in our society.

> It would be easy to blame the media for creating and maintaining many of the stereotypes with which the disabled still have to live. But the media only reflect attitudes that already exist in a body-beautiful society that tends to either ignore or ostracize people who don't measure up to the norm. This state of "invisibility" is particularly true for disabled women. (Israel & McPherson, 1983, pp. 4–15)

In a society that values the constructed image of health over health itself, a person with a disability does not fit the definition of healthy. In addition, since the person with a disability may be seen as representing a "failure" of modern medicine and health care (Matthews, 1983), there is no place for her or him in a book that promises people that they can attain health. The common attitude that disability and health are incompatible was expressed in its extreme by a faculty member who questioned the affirmative action statement in a position description for a health education faculty member; he wanted to know if encouraging "handicapped" people to apply was appropriate for a *health* education position.

Looking at the issue of health education and disabilities, it should be clear that it is easier for able-bodied people to be healthy, so more energy should be put into helping people with disabilities maximize their health. Able-bodied people often have more access to exercise, to rewarding work (economically[3] as well as emotionally), to leisure activities, and to health care facilities. Health care practitioners receive very little training about health issues relating to disability (self-care, sexual health), though they may receive information about specific pathologies, such as multiple sclerosis or muscular dystrophy. The inability to see, hear, or walk need not be the impairments to health they often are considered in our society. Health education is an obvious place to begin to change the societal attitudes toward disability that can help lead to poor physical and emotional health for disabled people. Health textbooks could present possibilities for change by showing ways that both disabled and able-bodied people can maximize health, and this could be done in both the text and the photographs. For example, one of those color chapter openers could include people with disabilities as healthy people. This might mean changing some of the representative "healthy" activities, such as windsurfing. While there are people with disabilities who participate in challenging and risky physical activities, there is no need for pressure to achieve *beyond* what would be expected of the able-bodied.[4] Showing a range of healthy activities that might be more accessible to both the physically disabled and the less physically active able-bodied would be appropriate.

Fat People

There are no fat people in the healthy-image photographs. Some people who agree with the rest of my analysis may here respond, "Of course not!" because there is a common assumption in our society that being thin is healthy and that any weight gain reduces health. In fact, evidence shows that being overweight (but not obese) is *not unhealthy.* In many cases, being very fat is a lot healthier than the ways people are encouraged to attempt to reduce weight—from extreme low-calorie diets, some of which are fatal, to stomach stapling and other surgeries

(Norsigian, 1986). In addition, dieting does not work for 99 percent of dieters, with 95 percent ending up heavier than before they started. Repeated dieting stresses the heart, as well as other organs (Norsigian, 1986). Our national obsession with thinness is certainly one factor leading to an unhealthy range of eating behaviors, including, but not limited to, bulimia and anorexia. While health textbooks warn against dangerous diets and "eating disorders," and encourage safe, sensible weight-loss diets, they do nothing to counter the image of thin as healthy.

Defining which people are "fat" in photographs is obviously problematic. In doing so, I am giving my subjective interpretation of what I see as society's definition of ideal weight. Those photographs I have identified as "fat" are of people who by common societal definitions would be seen as "needing to lose weight." In the United States most women are dissatisfied with their own body weight, so are more likely to place themselves in the "need to lose weight" category than to give that label to someone else of the same size.

Not counting people who were part of a crowd scene, I found 14 photographs that clearly showed people who were fat. One appeared in a chapter on the health care system with a caption referring to "lack of preventive maintenance leading to medical problems" (Carroll & Miller, 1986, p. 471), one in a chapter on drinking, and one under cardiovascular problems. The remaining 11 appeared in chapters on weight control or diet and nutrition. Of the 11, one was the "before" of "before and after" weight-loss photographs. One showed a woman walking briskly as part of a "fat-management program" (Mullen, Gold, Belcastro, & McDermott, 1986, p. 125); that was the most positive of the images. Most of the photographs were of people doing nothing but being fat or adding to that fat (eating or cooking). Three of the photographs showed women with children, referring by caption or topic heading to causes of obesity, either genetic or environmental. Only 3 of the 11 photographs were of men. In these photographs, it seems we are not being shown a person or an activity, but a disease—a disease called obesity that we all might "catch" if we don't carefully follow the prescriptions for health. Fat people's excess weight is seen as their fault for not following these prescriptions. This failure results from a lack of either willpower or restraint, as implied by the photographs that show fat people eating and thus both draw on and lend support to the myth that fat people eat too much. The only health problem of fat people is seen as their weight; if that were changed, all other problems would presumably disappear. As pointed out earlier, the health problems of losing excess weight, particularly in the yo-yo pattern of weight loss/gain, may be greater than those created by the extra weight. In addition, the emotional and mental health problems caused by our society's fatophobia may be more serious than the physical problems (Worcester, 1988). These texts strongly reinforce fatophobia by validating it with health "science."

Health educators who consciously work against racism and sexism should carefully reevaluate how our attitudes help perpetuate discrimination against all groups. As Nancy Worcester (1988) points out,

> The animosity towards fat people is such a fundamental part of our society, that people who have consciously worked on their other prejudices have not questioned their attitude towards body weight. People who would not think of laughing at a sexist or racist joke ridicule and make comments about fat people without recognizing that they are simply perpetuating another set of attitudes which negatively affect a whole group of people. (p. 234)

An alternative approach would be to recognize that people would be healthier if less pressure were put on them to lose weight. Fat people can benefit from exercise, if it is accessible and appropriate (low impact aerobics, for example), without the goal needing to be weight loss (Sternhell, 1985). Photographs of "not thin" people, involved in a variety of activities, could be scattered throughout the text, and the pictures of those labeled obese could be eliminated completely. We all know what an obese person looks like; we do not need to have that person held up as a symbol of both unhealthiness and lack of moral character.

Old People

The healthy-image photographs show people who appeared to be predominantly in their teens and twenties, which is the age group toward which these college texts would be geared. Rather subjectively, as with the issue of weight, I will describe as old[5] those who appear to be about 65 or older. Obviously I probably judged incorrectly on some photographs, but since the representations seem to be skewed toward the young or the old, with the middle-aged not so prominent, my task was relatively easy. I identified 84 photographs that contained people I classified as old. Of these, 52 appeared in chapters specifically on aging or growing older, 10 appeared in chapters on death and dying, and the remaining 22 were distributed in a wide range of topics. Of these 22, several still focused on the issue of age. For example, a photograph of an old heterosexual couple in a chapter entitled "Courtship and Marriage" is captioned, "While some people change partners repeatedly, many others spend their lifetime with a single spouse" (Carroll & Miller, 1986, p. 271). One text showed a similar photo and caption of a heterosexual couple, but also included an old gay male couple on the next page (Levy, Dignan, & Shirreffs, 1987). This represents an important step in terms of deghettoization of gay and lesbian images, and a broadening of views about sexuality and aging. Two photos showed old people as "non-traditional students"; another depicted a man running after recovering from a stroke; and yet another featured George Burns as a representative of someone who has lived a long life. In others of the 22, the age is incidental, as in a man painting (mental health), people shopping in an open market (nutrition), people walking (fitness), a man smoking.

As the societally stereotyped *appearance* of health diminishes, as occurs with aging, it is assumed that health unavoidably diminishes. In fact, while there is some inevitable biological decline with age, many health problems can be averted by good nutrition, exercise, and preventive health care. Many of the health problems of aging have economic, rather than biological, causes, such as lack of appropriate health insurance coverage (Sidel, 1986). In a society that is afraid to face aging, people may not be able to accept that they will experience the effects of aging that they so carefully avoid (if they are lucky enough to live that long). In addition, as with disability, the people who may need to do more to maintain health are those being most ignored.

It is significant that these texts have sections on aging, which contain many positive images, but it is also crucial that health be seen as something that can be attained and maintained by people of all ages. The attempt to include representations of aging in these books must be expanded so that people of all ages are seen to be able to be healthy—a state now seemingly, in those images of health, to be enjoyed only by the young.

Urban Setting

The healthy-image photographs showing outdoor scenes are situated at the beach or in other nonurban settings; it is possible some were set in city parks, but there are no urban markers in the photographs. Bike riding, running, kicking a soccer ball, playing volleyball can all be done in urban settings, though the hang gliding and sky diving would obviously be difficult. Considering the high percentage of the U.S. population that lives in cities (and the numbers of those that cannot easily get out), it seems that urban settings should be represented in the texts. Of the 28 other photographs I identified as clearly having urban settings, I could see only 4 as positive. Two of these showed outdoor vegetable/fruit markets, one showed bike riding as a way of both reducing pollution and getting exercise in the city, and one showed a family playing ball together.

Of the rest, 9 appeared in chapters on the environment, with negative images of urban decay, smog, and crowded streets; 10 were in chapters on mental health or stress, showing scenes representing loneliness, stress, or anger, such as a crowded subway or a potential fight on a street corner. Drinking and drug chapters had two urban scenes: "skid row" alcoholics and an apparently drunk man unconscious on the street. There were also three urban scenes in sexuality chapters—two of streets with marquees for sex shows and one showing a "man 'flashing' Central Park" (Payne & Hahn, 1986, p. 348).

There is a clear message that it is unhealthy to live in the city. While this is partly true—that is, the city may have increased pollution of various kinds, specific stresses, less access to certain forms of exercise, and other problems—there are healthy ways to live in a city. One of the roles of health education should be to help us recognize healthier options within the limits imposed on us by economic or other factors. Rather than conveying the message that urban dwelling inevitably condemns people to ill health (unless they can afford to get away periodically to the beach or the mountains), scenes showing health within the city could be presented.

Options for positive images include scenes of outdoor activities in what are clearly city parks, people enjoying cultural events found more easily in cities, gardening in a vacant lot, or a neighborhood block party. Urban settings are excellent for representing walking as a healthy activity. City dwellers are more likely to walk to work, to shopping, and to social activities than are suburbanites, many of whom habitually drive. Urban walking can be presented as free, accessible, and healthy in terms of exercise, stress reduction, and reducing pollution. More indoor activities could be shown so that the external environment is not seen as a determinant of "healthy" activity. These might give a sense of the possibilities for health within what otherwise might appear to be a very dirty, dangerous, stressful place to be.

Work and Leisure

The healthy-image photographs I analyzed were all associated with leisure activities, so I tried to establish how these texts represent work in relationship to health. For this analysis, all photographs of health care workers were excluded, since these are used predominantly to illustrate health or medical issues. Of the 16 other photographs showing people at work, 4 were related to discussions of sex roles and women doing nontraditional work (phone "lineman," lawyer). This seems part of a positive trend in textbooks to reduce sexism. An obvious next step would be to show women in nontraditional work roles without commenting on them, as is done with a number of photographs of women as doctors. Six of the photographs of work accompany discussions of stress. Besides stress, there are no illustrations of health hazards at work except for one photograph of a farm worker being sprayed with pesticides. Three positive references to work show someone working at a computer (illustrating self-development), a man in a wheelchair doing carpentry, and an old man continuing to work.

Overall, the number of photographs representing work seems low, considering the amount of time we put into work during a lifetime. Blue-collar work is represented by trash collectors in an environmental health section, police officers in a weight control chapter, firefighters under stress, a construction worker in the opener for a stress chapter, the farm worker mentioned above, and women in nontraditional work. Blue-collar work is seen in terms of neither potential health hazards beyond stress nor the positive health aspects of working. The strongest connection between health and work presented involves the stress of white-collar jobs (symbolized by a man at a desk talking on the phone). The message seems to be that health is not affected by work, unless it is emotionally stressful.

The photographs in this book seem to be aimed at middle-class students who assume they will become white-collar workers or professionals who can afford leisure activities, both in terms of time and money. Those who work in obviously physically dangerous jobs, such as construction work, or in jobs that have stress as only one of many health hazards, are rarely portrayed. These people are also likely not to be able to afford recreation such as hang gliding (and also might not need the stimulus of physical risk taking if their job is physically risky in itself). These photographs serve to compartmentalize work as if it were not part of life and not relevant to health.

Rather than selecting photographs that reinforce the work–leisure split and the alienation of the worker from work, editors could include photographs that show the health rewards of work and the real health risks of a wide variety of work. For example, a photograph of a group of workers talking on a lunch break could be captioned, "Many people find strong support networks among their co-workers." Another photograph could be of a union meeting, illustrating that work-related stress is reduced when we have more control over the conditions of our work. In addition the mental health benefits of a rewarding job might be emphasized, perhaps in contrast with the stress of unemployment. Health risks, and ways to minimize them, could be illustrated with photographs ranging from typists using video display terminals to mine workers. A very important addition would be inclusion in the healthy-image photographs of some representation of work.

CONCLUSION

The definition of health that emerges from an examination of the healthy-image photographs is very narrow. The healthy person is young, slim, white, physically abled, physically active, and, apparently, comfortable financially. Since these books are trying to "sell" their images of health to college students, the photographs presumably can be seen as representing people whom the students would wish to become. Some students, however, cannot or may not wish to become part of this vision of the healthy person. For example, students of color may feel alienated by this all-white vision. What may be most problematic is that in defining the healthy person, these photographs also define *who can become healthy*. By this definition many are excluded from the potential for health: people who are physically disabled, no longer young, not slim (unless they can lose weight, even if in unhealthy ways), urban dwellers, poor people, and people of color. For various social, economic, and political reasons, these may be among the least healthy groups in the United States, but the potential for health is there if the health care and health education systems do not disenfranchise them.

The healthy-image photographs represent the healthy lifestyle, not in the sense of the lifestyle that will help someone attain health, but the white, middle-class, heterosexual, leisure, active lifestyle that is the reward of attaining health. These glowing images imitate common advertising representations. An ice chest of beer would not be out of place next to the volleyball players on the beach, and a soft drink slogan would fit well with the windsurfers or sky divers. It must be remembered, however, that while college students may be the market for beer, soft drinks, and "health," they are not the market for textbooks. Obviously, the biggest single factor affecting a student's purchase of a text is whether it is required. The decision may also be based on how much reading in the book is assigned, whether exam questions will be drawn from the text, its potential future usefulness, or its resale value.

The market for textbooks is the faculty who make text selections for courses (Coser, Kadushin, & Powell, 1982). While the photographs may be designed to create in students a desire for health, they are also there to sell health educators the book. Therefore, health educators should take some time examining the representations in these texts, while questioning their own definitions of who is healthy and who can become healthy. Do they actually wish to imply that access to health is limited to young, white, slim, middle-class, physically abled, and physically active people? If health educators are committed to increasing the potential for health for *all* people, then the focus should not be directed primarily at those for whom health is most easily attained and maintained. Rethinking the images that represent health may help restructure health educators' goals.

It is an interesting exercise to try to envision alternative healthy-image photographs. Here is one of my choices for a cover photograph: An old woman of color, sitting on a chair with a book in her lap, is looking out at a small garden that has been reclaimed from an urban backlot.

Acknowledgments. I would like to thank Nancy Worcester, Julie D'Acci, Sally Lesher, and Elizabeth Ellsworth for their critical readings of this chapter and their valuable suggestions.

NOTES

1. Cars appear in health textbook photographs primarily in the context of either environmental concerns or the stresses of modern life.

2. Occasionally, photographs used were actually taken for advertising purposes. For example, in a chapter on exercise there is a full-page color photograph of a runner with the credit "Photo by Jerry LaRocca for Nike" (Insel & Roth, 1988, p. 316).

3. Examining the wages of disabled women can give a sense of the potential economic problems: "The 1981 Census revealed that disabled women earn less than 24 cents for each dollar earned by nondisabled men; black disabled women earn 12 cents for each dollar. Disabled women earn approximately 52 percent of what nondisabled women earn" (Saxton & Howe, 1987, p. xii).

4. "Supercrip" is a term sometimes used among people with disabilities to describe people with disabilities who go beyond what would be expected of those with no disabilities. It should not be necessary to be a one-legged ski champion or a blind physician to prove that people with disabilities deserve the opportunities available to the able-bodied. By emphasizing the individual "heroes," the focus shifts away from societal barriers and obstacles to individual responsibility to excel.

5. I am using "old" rather than "older" for two reasons that have been identified by many writing about ageism. "Older" seems a euphemism that attempts to lessen the impact of discussing someone's age, along with such terms as senior citizen or golden ager. The second point is the simple question: "Older than whom?"

REFERENCES

Barsky, A. J. (1988). The paradox of health. *The New England Journal of Medicine, 318* (7), 414–418.

Barthes, R. (1977). *Image-music-text.* (S. Heath, Trans.). New York: Hill and Wang.

Berger, J. (1972). *Ways of seeing.* London: British Broadcasting Corporation and Penguin Books.

Coser, L. A., Kadushin, C., & Powell, W. (1982). *Books: The culture and commerce of publishing.* New York: Basic Books.

Israel, P., & McPherson, C. (1983). Introduction. In G. F. Matthews, *Voices from the shadows: Women with disabilities speak out* (pp. 13–21). Toronto: Women's Educational Press.

Leiss, W., Kline, S., & Jhally, S. (1986). *Social communication in advertising: Persons, products and images of well-being.* Toronto: Methuen.

Matthews, G. F. (1983). *Voices from the shadows: Women with disabilities speak out.* Toronto: Women's Educational Press.

Norsigian, J. (1986, May/June). Dieting is dangerous to your health. *The Network News.* National Women's Health Network, 4, 6.

Overman, S. J., Mimms, S. E., & Harris, J. B. (1987). Readability of selected college personal health textbooks. *Health Education, 18* (4), 28–30.

Saxton, M., & Howe, F. (Eds.). (1987). *With wings: An anthology of literature by and about women with disabilities.* New York: Feminist Press at the City University of New York.

Sidel, R. (1986). *Women and children last.* New York: Viking Penguin.

Sternhell, C. (1985, May). We'll always be fat but fat can be fit. *Ms.,* pp. 66–68, 141, 154.

Whatley, M. H. (1988). Photographic images of blacks in sexuality texts. *Curriculum Inquiry, 18* (2), 137–155.

Worcester, N. (1988). Fatophobia. In N. Worcester & M. H. Whatley (Eds.), *Women's health: Readings on social, economic, and political issues.* Dubuque, IA: Kendall/Hunt.

Worcester, N., & Whatley, M. H. (1988). The response of the health care system to the women's health movement. In S. Rosser (Ed.), *Feminism within the science and health care professions: Overcoming resistance* (pp. 117–130). New York: Pergamon.

APPENDIX:
TEXTBOOKS EXAMINED FOR THIS CHAPTER

Carroll, C., & Miller, D. (1986). *Health: The science of human adaptation* (4th ed.). Dubuque, IA: Wm. C. Brown.

Dintiman, G. B., & Greenberg, J. (1986). *Health through discovery* (3rd ed.). New York: Random House.

Hales, D. R., & Williams, B. K. (1986). *An invitation to health: Your personal responsibility* (3rd ed.). Menlo Park, CA: Benjamin/Cummings Publishing Company.

Insel, P. M., & Roth, W. T. (1988). *Core concepts in health* (5th ed.). Mountain View, CA: Mayfield Publishing.

Levy, M. R., Dignan, M., & Shirreffs, J. H. (1987). *Life and health.* (5th ed.). New York: Random House.

Mullen, K. D., Gold, R. S., Belcastro, P. A., & McDermott, R. J. (1986). *Connections for health.* Dubuque, IA: Wm. C. Brown.

Payne, W. A., & Hahn, D. B. (1986). *Understanding your health,* St. Louis: Times Mirror/Mosby.

About the Contributors

ANN DE VANEY is a professor in the Department of Curriculum and Instruction and head of the Educational Communications and Technology Program at the University of Wisconsin—Madison. Her research addresses the structure of television, and media and gender.

ELIZABETH ELLSWORTH is an associate professor in the Department of Curriculum and Instruction and a member of the Women's Studies Program at the University of Wisconsin—Madison. Her work focuses on educational media and social change, and on the ideology of educational films and videos. Among her most recent publications are "Why Doesn't This Feel Empowering? Working Through the Repressive Myths of Critical Pedagogy" (*Harvard Educational Review*, 55 (3), 297–324), "Educational Films Against Critical Pedagogy" (*Journal of Education, 169* (3), 32–47), and "I Pledge Allegiance: The Politics of Reading and Using Educational Documentaries" (*Curriculum Inquiry*, in press).

BARBARA ERDMAN is an assistant professor at Ohio State University in the Department of Educational Policy and Leadership, where she teaches in the Instructional Design and Technology program area. Her research interests include aesthetics and the design of educational media.

MARGOT KENNARD is a research associate in the Education Services Area of Wisconsin Public Television. She has a Ph.D. in educational communications technology with an emphasis in women's studies and media production. Currently, her research investigates interaction in teleconferencing and distance learning.

MIMI ORNER is a doctoral candidate in the Department of Curriculum and Instruction at the University of Wisconsin—Madison, where she both teaches and produces educational video. Her research focuses on the politics of media access and representation regarding race, class, and gender.

BONNIE K. TRUDELL is an assistant professor in the Department of Curriculum and Instruction and a member of the Women's Studies Program at the University of Wisconsin—Madison. She has an M.S. in child and family studies and a Ph.D. in curriculum and instruction from UW—Madison, having returned to earn the doctorate after two decades of involvement in health and sexuality education as a classroom teacher, curriculum consultant, community educator, and workshop facilitator. Her research involves illumination of the day-to-day classroom process by which school knowledge about health and sexuality is constructed. She has examined the unintended consequences and dilemmas that prepackaged curricular materials raise for classroom teachers, their accommodation and resistance to such material, and factors influencing their curricular decisions. She has co-authored, with Mariamne Whatley, articles on school sexual abuse prevention in *International Journal of Child Abuse and Neglect, Journal of Education,* and *Theory into Practice.*

MARIAMNE H. WHATLEY is an associate professor at the University of Wisconsin—Madison, with a joint appointment between the Department of Curriculum and Instruction and the Women's Studies Program. After completing her undergraduate degree in English at Radcliffe College, she received her Ph.D. in biological science from Northwestern University. She currently teaches women's health and biology, and health education. Her research brings a feminist perspective both to women's health issues and to sexuality/health education.

Index